MAKER COMICS

FIX A CAR!

1

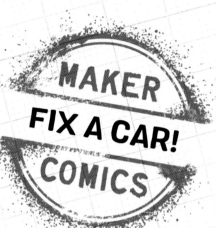

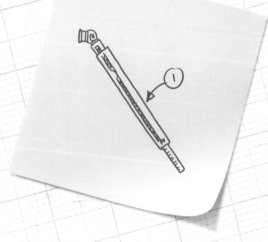

FIX A CAR!

Chris Schweizer

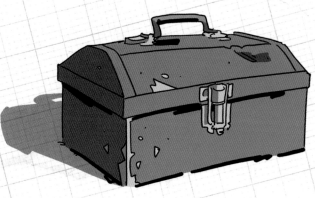

:01
First Second
New York

Working on cars can be a great experience, but only if you do so **carefully**! Cars are heavy, complicated objects that have fast moving parts and dangerous chemicals, so always be diligent about safety!

Be sure to pay attention to the safety notes throughout the book. Read the packaging of any oils, fluids, or other products you use so you know how to handle them and dispose of them safely.

Follow instructions carefully when touching anything under the hood. Certain surfaces may be hot or corrosive.

Never allow an engine to run in a closed space (like a garage with the door shut). You can't see or smell the carbon monoxide in car exhaust, but it's deadly.

Cars have been known to fall off jacks. Never put your body, **or any part of your body**, under a car that is suspended on a jack.

Car repairs are easier and safer when you have an experienced helper. Make sure that an adult is on hand whenever you're doing repairs.

And when you go for a ride, **always** buckle your seat belt!

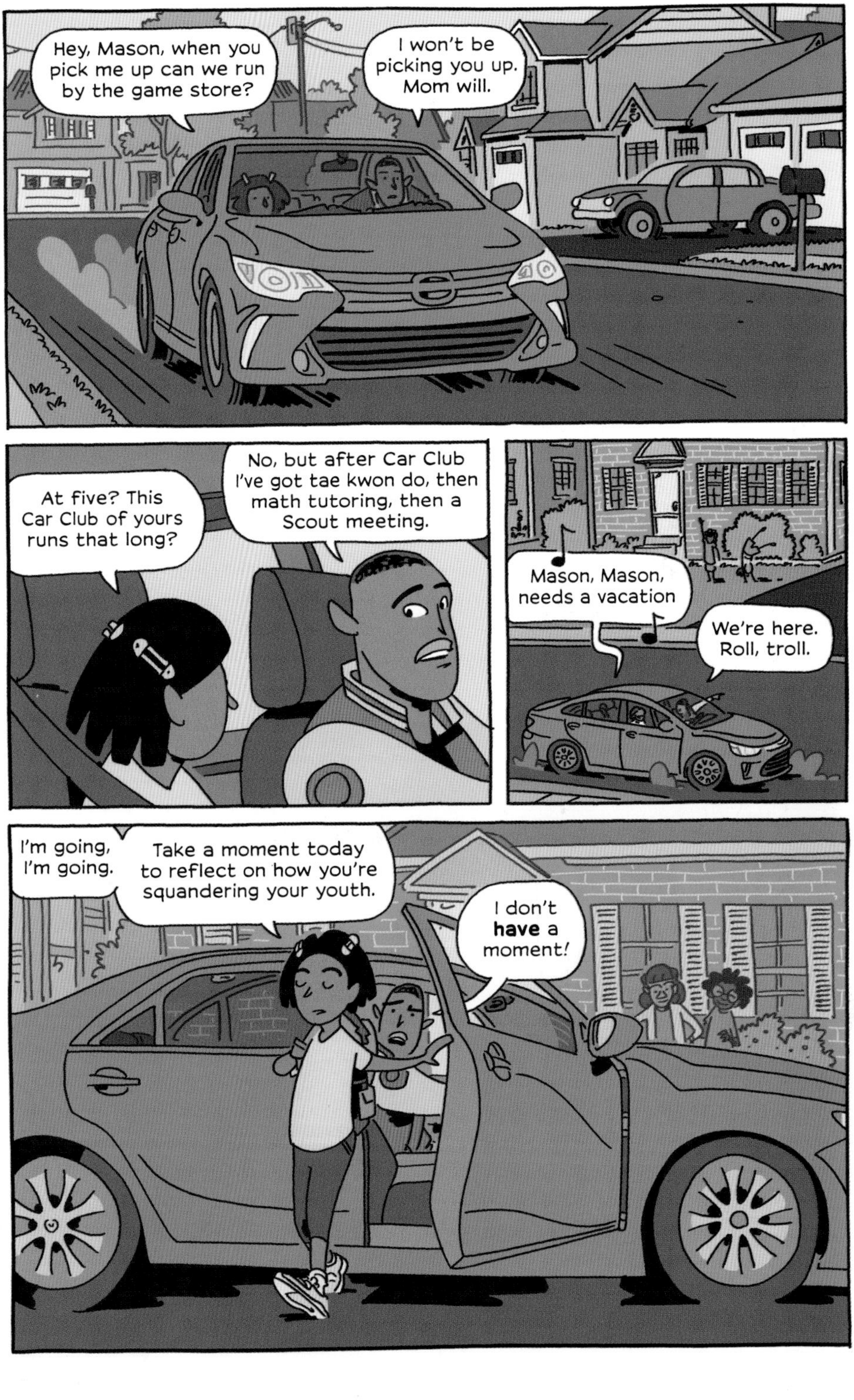
Hey, Mason, when you pick me up can we run by the game store?
I won't be picking you up. Mom will.
At five? This Car Club of yours runs that long?
No, but after Car Club I've got tae kwon do, then math tutoring, then a Scout meeting.
Mason, Mason, needs a vacation
We're here. Roll, troll.
I'm going, I'm going.
Take a moment today to reflect on how you're squandering your youth.
I don't **have** a moment!

-RING-

-RI~

Hey, Ma.

Lena, have you gotten to Car Club yet?

Not yet. I'm taking a scenic route.

Well, make sure you follow the speed limit.

Don't worry, Ma...

...I'm not going a bit over thirty-five.

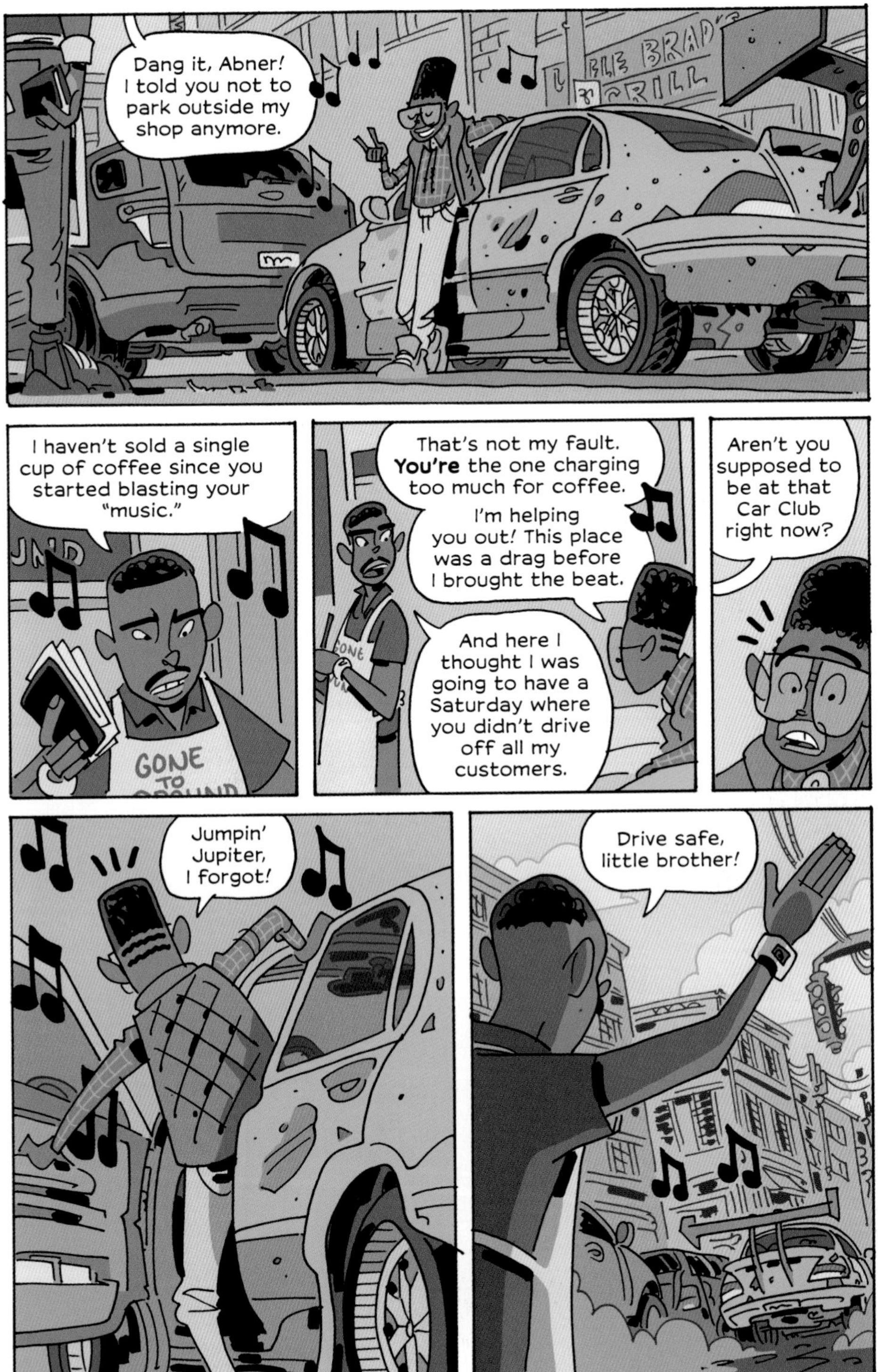
Dang it, Abner! I told you not to park outside my shop anymore.
BIG BRAD'S GRILL
I haven't sold a single cup of coffee since you started blasting your "music."
GONE TO GROUND
That's not my fault. **You're** the one charging too much for coffee.
I'm helping you out! This place was a drag before I brought the beat.
And here I thought I was going to have a Saturday where you didn't drive off all my customers.
Aren't you supposed to be at that Car Club right now?
Jumpin' Jupiter, I forgot!
Drive safe, little brother!

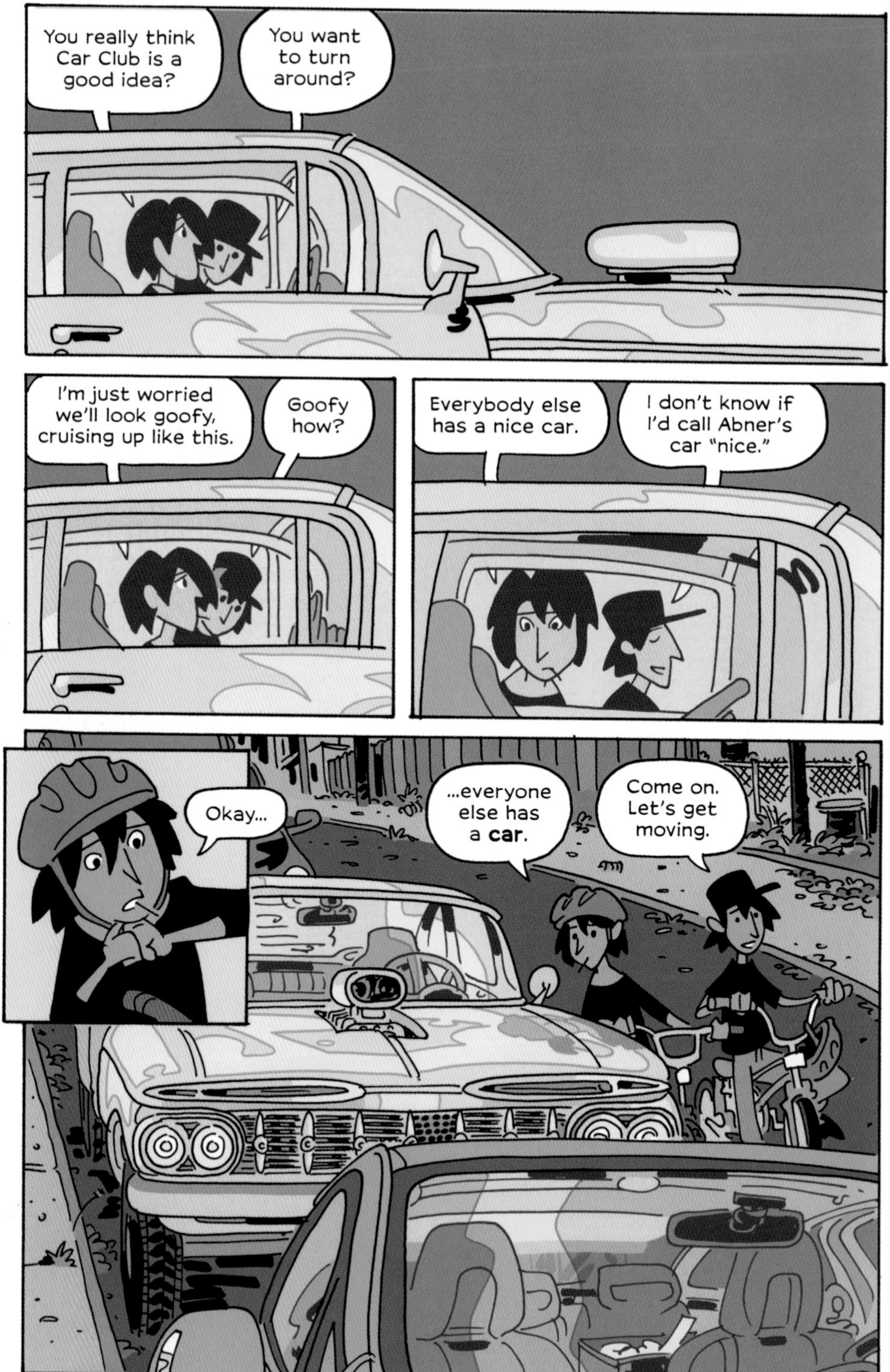

You really think Car Club is a good idea?
You want to turn around?
I'm just worried we'll look goofy, cruising up like this.
Goofy how?
Everybody else has a nice car.
I don't know if I'd call Abner's car "nice."
Okay...
...everyone else has a **car**.
Come on. Let's get moving.

All right, youngsters...

Welcome to **Car Club**!

Thanks, Ms. Gritt.

Yeah, we're pumped you're doing this.

Are you kidding? The only thing I enjoy more than **teaching** is taking care of **cars**...

...and the only thing I enjoy more than taking care of cars is teaching **others** how to **do** it.

Aw, I **know** how to take care of a car, Ms. G.

I'm here 'cause your garage is supposed to be a real sock-knocker.

I heard that, too.

Well, I **am** mighty proud of it.

Guess I **could** show it off.

All right!

5

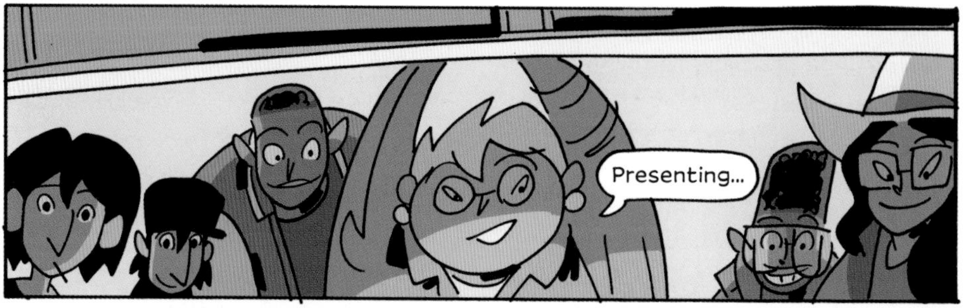
Presenting...

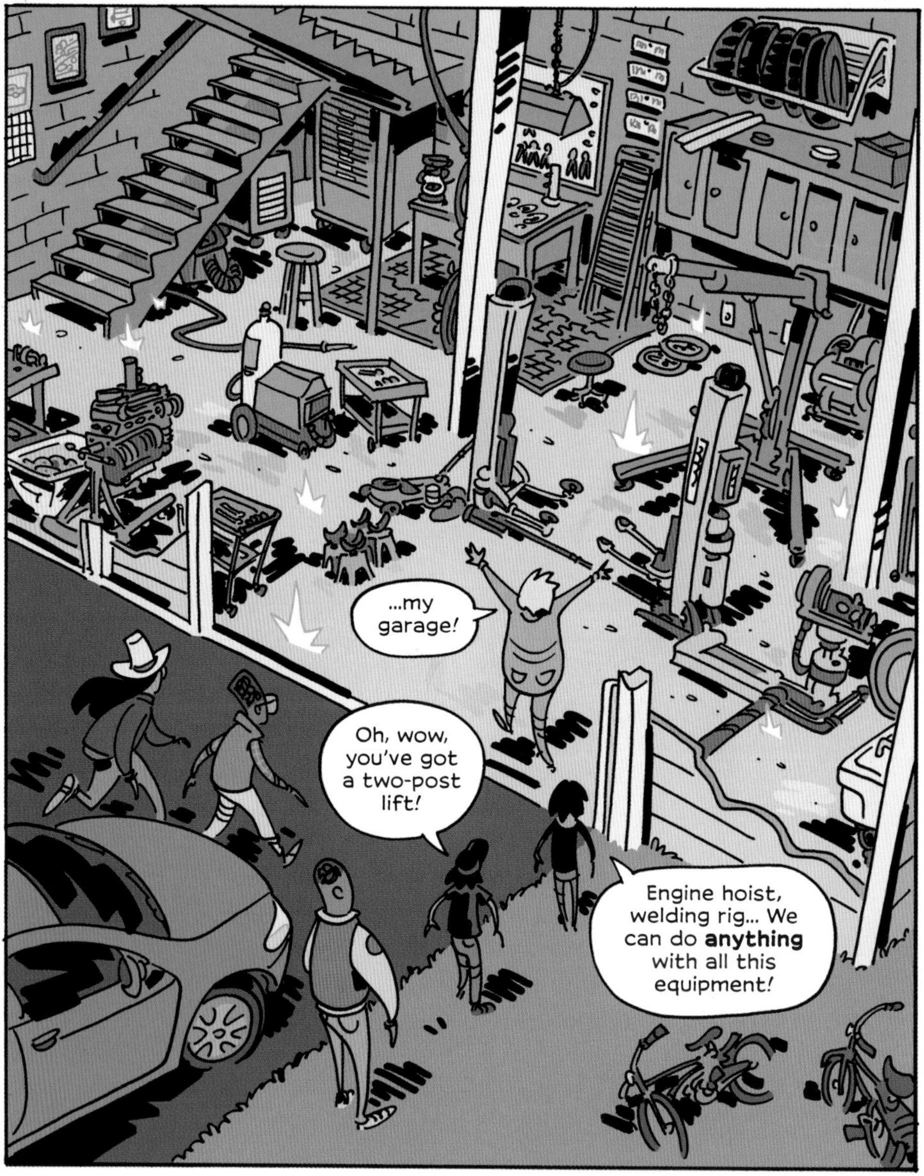
...my garage!
Oh, wow, you've got a two-post lift!
Engine hoist, welding rig... We can do **anything** with all this equipment!

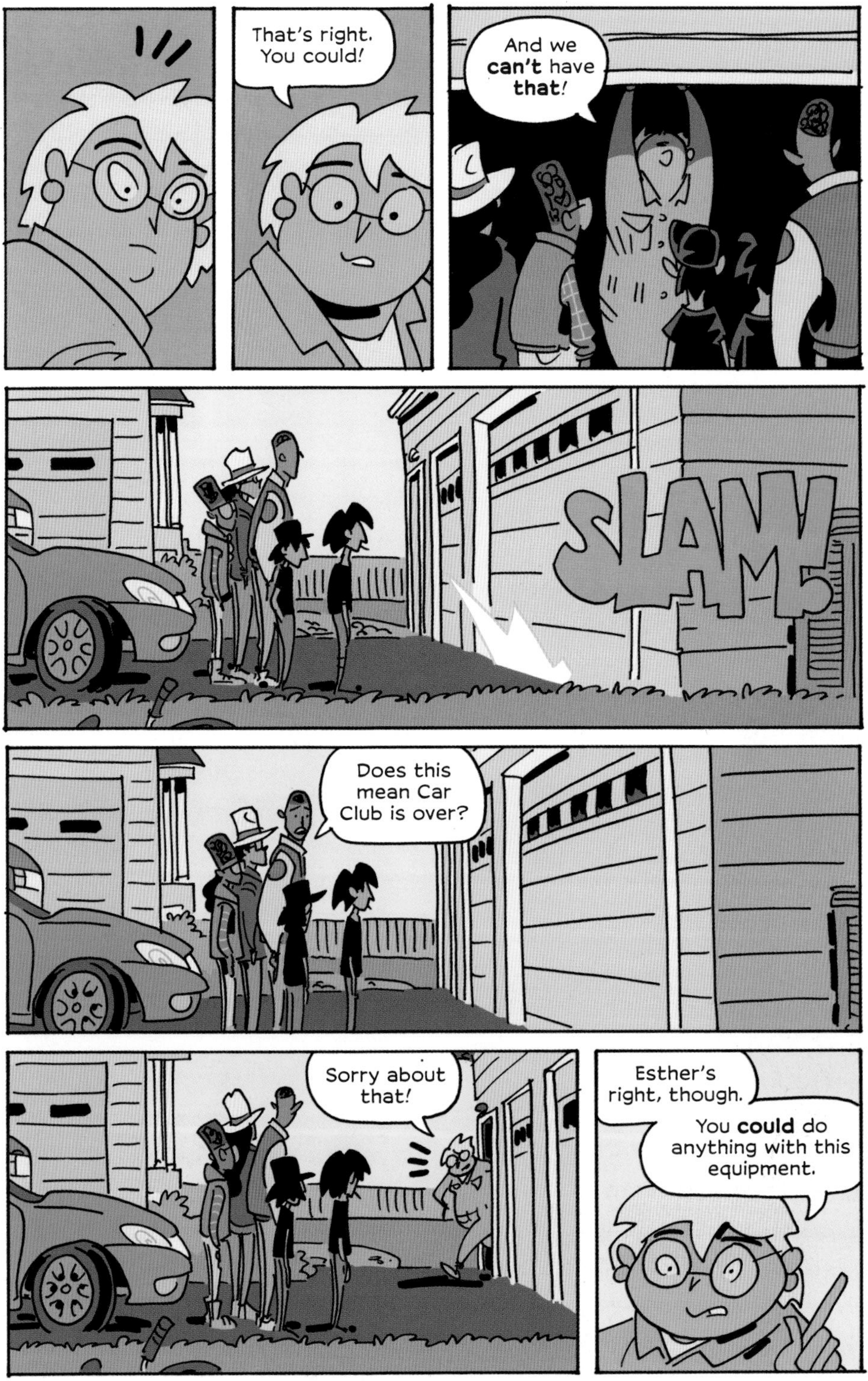
That's right. You could!
And we **can't** have **that**!
SLAM
Does this mean Car Club is over?
Sorry about that!
Esther's right, though.
You **could** do anything with this equipment.

Which would defeat the purpose of Car Club!

The whole point of this endeavor is to help you learn how to take care of cars on your own.

But how are we supposed to take care of cars without any equipment?

You don't need a big, fancy garage like mine.

Most of the repairs and maintenance you'll be learning only require a few simple, affordable tools.

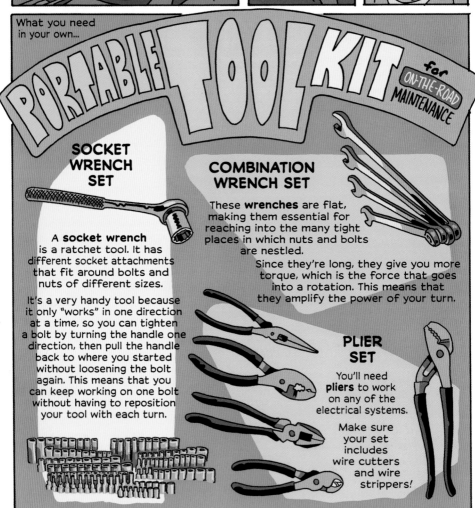

What you need in your own...

PORTABLE TOOL KIT for ON-THE-ROAD MAINTENANCE

SOCKET WRENCH SET

A **socket wrench** is a ratchet tool. It has different socket attachments that fit around bolts and nuts of different sizes.

It's a very handy tool because it only "works" in one direction at a time, so you can tighten a bolt by turning the handle one direction, then pull the handle back to where you started without loosening the bolt again. This means that you can keep working on one bolt without having to reposition your tool with each turn.

COMBINATION WRENCH SET

These **wrenches** are flat, making them essential for reaching into the many tight places in which nuts and bolts are nestled.

Since they're long, they give you more torque, which is the force that goes into a rotation. This means that they amplify the power of your turn.

PLIER SET

You'll need **pliers** to work on any of the electrical systems.

Make sure your set includes wire cutters and wire strippers!

8

BREAKER BAR

Sometimes bolts have been on too long or are just too tight to take off with a combination wrench or a socket wrench. A mechanic might use power tools, but with a little bit of effort, a **breaker bar** can get even the toughest bolt moving.

It's a lot like a socket wrench, but the longer handle offers a lot more torque, and the end is fixed (meaning it doesn't ratchet like a socket wrench). It still uses the same sockets, though!

SCREWDRIVERS

There are a lot of pieces in the car that require a **screwdriver** to take off (and put back!). You'll need Phillips and flathead types, both regular size and stubby for those tight places. You'll also want tiny ones for electronics work and a long flathead screwdriver that you can also use as a pry bar to separate parts that have gotten stuck together.

AUTOMOTIVE JACK

A **jack** lifts the car off the ground. Many cars come with jacks, so there's a good chance that you might already have one folded up under the back seat or under a panel in the trunk.

You'll need a jack to change a tire, but if you want to do more than that, you'll need to get **jack stands,** too. Working on a car being held up by just a jack can be **very** unsafe, and the only time you should do it is when changing a tire.

You'll also want...

ELECTRICAL TAPE

...for emergency repairs on wires and hoses!

A HEADLAMP & A FLASHLIGHT

...to see into a dark engine and underneath the car!

GLOVES

...to protect your hands!

Some of the work you'll be doing might require other tools, but those give you a great start.

You can keep them in your car for emergency repairs. Except for the breaker bar and the jack, they'll all fit in a tackle box, toolbox, or small laundry bin.

But you know what? You'll have a lot **fewer** emergency repairs **if** you pay attention to our **first lesson**.

What's the first lesson?

THE FIRST LESSON: PREVENTIVE MAINTENANCE

If you check your car's systems regularly, you can catch little problems before they become big ones!

That's what we'll be doing today.

Catching little problems?

Maybe!

We're going to learn about what the different systems do.

Once we understand **that**, it's easy to make sure that they're doing what they're supposed to!

So let's start with **fluids**.

Fluids are the easiest part of your car to check.

Mason, could you pop your hood for me?

There are **six** fluids that you can check in most cars.

But there are only **four** here.

Oil, washer fluid, brake fluid, and **coolant**.

Oil fill cap

Brake fluid

Windshield washer fluid

Oil level dipstick

Engine coolant

The other two are **transmission fluid** and **power steering fluid**.

This is a newer model car. Many new cars have electric power steering and don't have an easy way to check the transmission fluid the way you can in older cars.

Don't worry, we'll look at **those** in **Abner's** car.

Oh yeah!

11

The first thing you ought to do is check the oil.

Your car engine has lots of moving parts, and almost all of these parts are made of **metal**.

Some parts move **thousands** of times **every minute.** If they were to grind against each other, these parts would wear out very quickly!

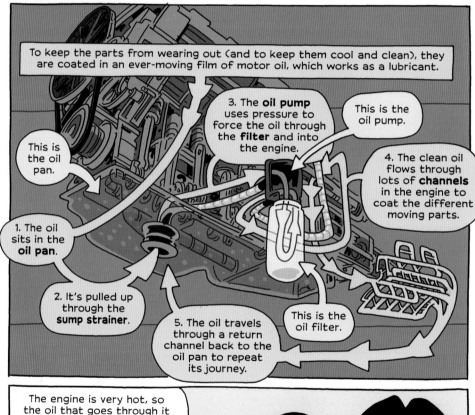

To keep the parts from wearing out (and to keep them cool and clean), they are coated in an ever-moving film of motor oil, which works as a lubricant.

3. The **oil pump** uses pressure to force the oil through the **filter** and into the engine.

This is the oil pump.

This is the oil pan.

4. The clean oil flows through lots of **channels** in the engine to coat the different moving parts.

1. The oil sits in the **oil pan**.

2. It's pulled up through the **sump strainer**.

5. The oil travels through a return channel back to the oil pan to repeat its journey.

This is the oil filter.

The engine is very hot, so the oil that goes through it eventually gets cooked away.

And if your engine is older, it will burn through oil faster than a new one.

Checking your oil level is easy. You just look for the **dipstick**.

The dipstick is a long, flat piece of metal that ends in a ring.

Every type of car is different, so if you have trouble finding your dipstick, check the owner's manual.

If you don't have a manual in your glove compartment, you can usually find it online.

Using the ring, pull the dipstick from its tube.

Wipe the oil off the dipstick with a rag or a paper towel.

Once you've wiped it clean, insert the dipstick **all the way** back into its tube.

Then you pull it out again.

Man, this is like the Hokey Pokey.

"You put the dipstick in, you take the dipstick out, you put the dipstick in, and you shake it all about..."

You better **not** shake it all about.

You splatter oil on my jacket, I'm gonna bring the thunder.

Now you can check the oil level.

The dipstick will have markings on it. There will be one mark near the end of the dipstick that says "add," and another a little ways up that will say "safe" or "full."

ADD! SAFE! DO NOT OVERFILL

Sometimes, instead of words, there will just be two holes or bumps. The one at the end means "add," and the other means "full."

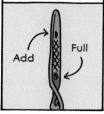

Add   Full

If your oil is under the "full" mark, it means that your car doesn't have enough oil in it to do its job.

If the oil on the dipstick looks like a golden-brown syrup, then you can simply add more oil when your level is low.

If it looks black, then it might be time to change it. Check to see if you're due for an oil change.*

Also pay attention if your oil appears foamy or creamy. This might just be due to changes in weather or condensation from driving infrequently, but it could mean that your coolant is mixing with the oil. If this is the case, you might have a leaky head gasket. You'll want to get that fixed so that your car doesn't overheat.

A lot of people check their oil level when they've stopped for gas, but that's not a good time because you've been driving.

It's important to let your car cool down for at least ten minutes before checking the oil level.

Otherwise the oil that's been running through the engine doesn't have time to drip back into the oil pan, and you might get a false low reading.

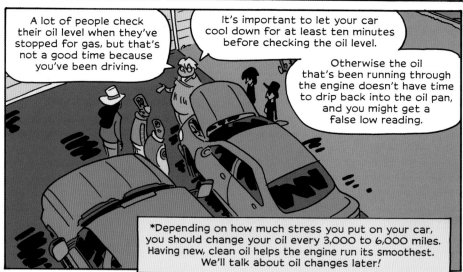

*Depending on how much stress you put on your car, you should change your oil every 3,000 to 6,000 miles. Having new, clean oil helps the engine run its smoothest. We'll talk about oil changes later!

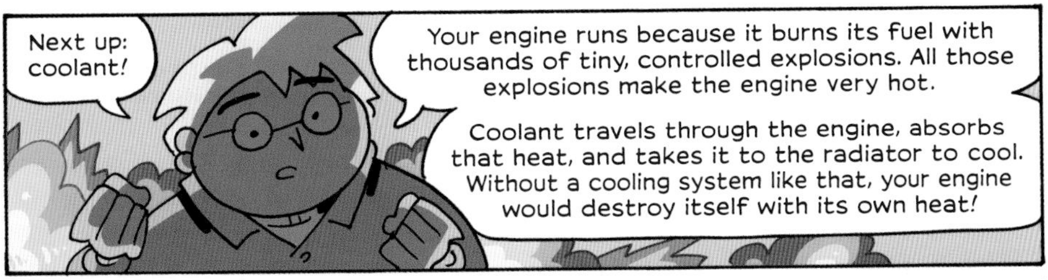
Next up: coolant!
Your engine runs because it burns its fuel with thousands of tiny, controlled explosions. All those explosions make the engine very hot.
Coolant travels through the engine, absorbs that heat, and takes it to the radiator to cool. Without a cooling system like that, your engine would destroy itself with its own heat!

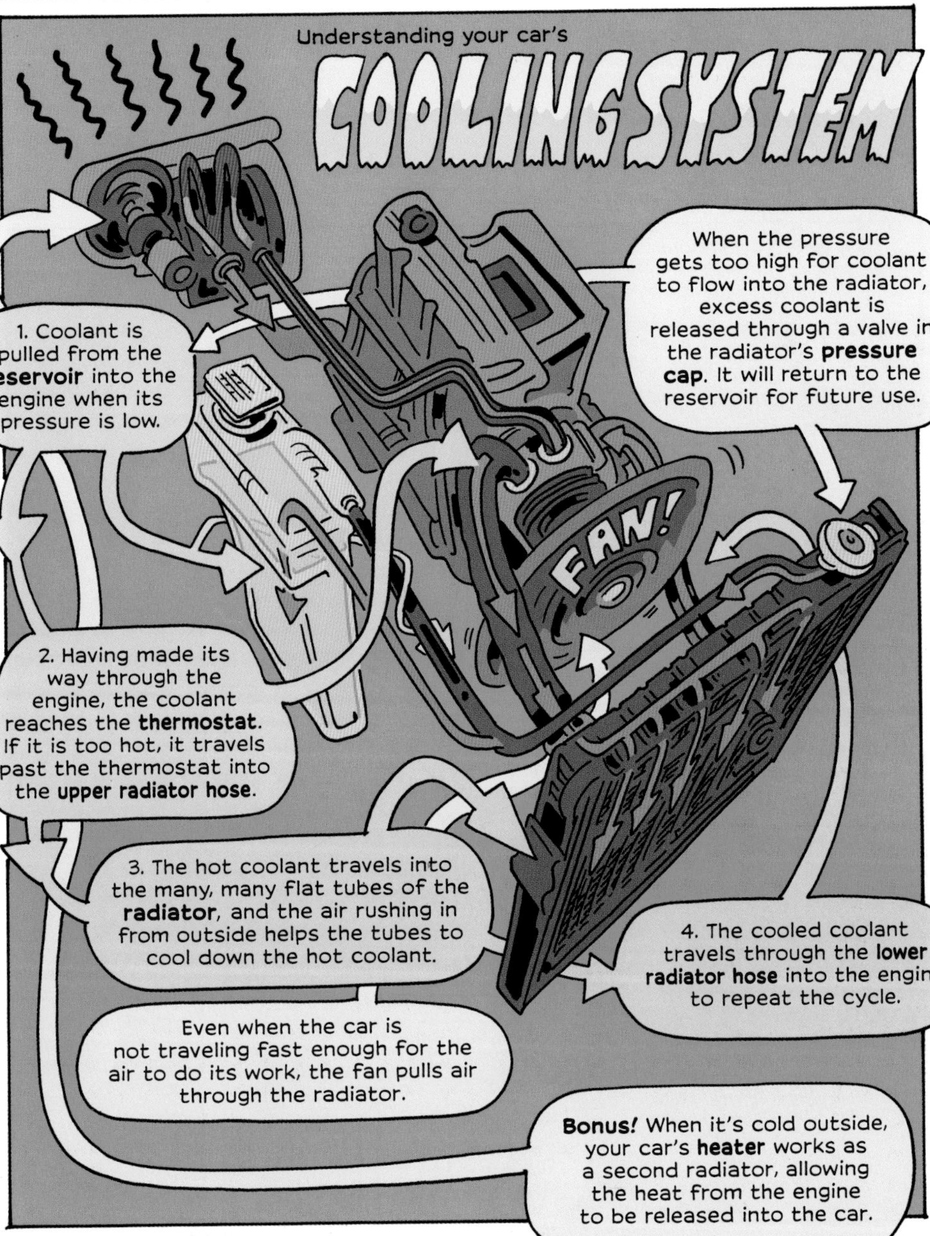
Understanding your car's
COOLING SYSTEM
1. Coolant is pulled from the **reservoir** into the engine when its pressure is low.
When the pressure gets too high for coolant to flow into the radiator, excess coolant is released through a valve in the radiator's **pressure cap**. It will return to the reservoir for future use.
FAN!
2. Having made its way through the engine, the coolant reaches the **thermostat**. If it is too hot, it travels past the thermostat into the **upper radiator hose**.
3. The hot coolant travels into the many, many flat tubes of the **radiator**, and the air rushing in from outside helps the tubes to cool down the hot coolant.
4. The cooled coolant travels through the **lower radiator hose** into the engine to repeat the cycle.
Even when the car is not traveling fast enough for the air to do its work, the fan pulls air through the radiator.
Bonus! When it's cold outside, your car's **heater** works as a second radiator, allowing the heat from the engine to be released into the car.

To make sure you have enough coolant, check the reservoir.

It's made of hard plastic, so it's pretty sturdy, but be careful when working around it. Plastic is easy to crack.

Never open the reservoir cap unless your car has had time to cool. Otherwise you could be hit in the face with scalding, toxic steam. Nobody wants that!

The reservoir should have markings that will let you know if it's low.

The coolant that you use is called **antifreeze**. It has a higher boiling point and a lower freezing point than water, so it will keep your car running smoothly even in very cold or very hot weather.

Pure antifreeze doesn't transfer heat as well as antifreeze mixed fifty-fifty with water does.

Some antifreeze comes premixed. **Be sure to read the label** to know whether or not to add water!

When you **do** need to add antifreeze, you add it to the reservoir. Be sure to use a funnel when pouring!

Funnels are for chumps!

My hands are **crazy** steady.

Years of gaming.

I don't **need** a funnel to make a clean pour.

Well, antifreeze is **very** poisonous. It's also very **sweet**.

If some gets on the ground, it might attract dogs, who will lap it up.

My hands are steady, too, but I wouldn't bet a pet's life on it.

Funnels are **all right**.

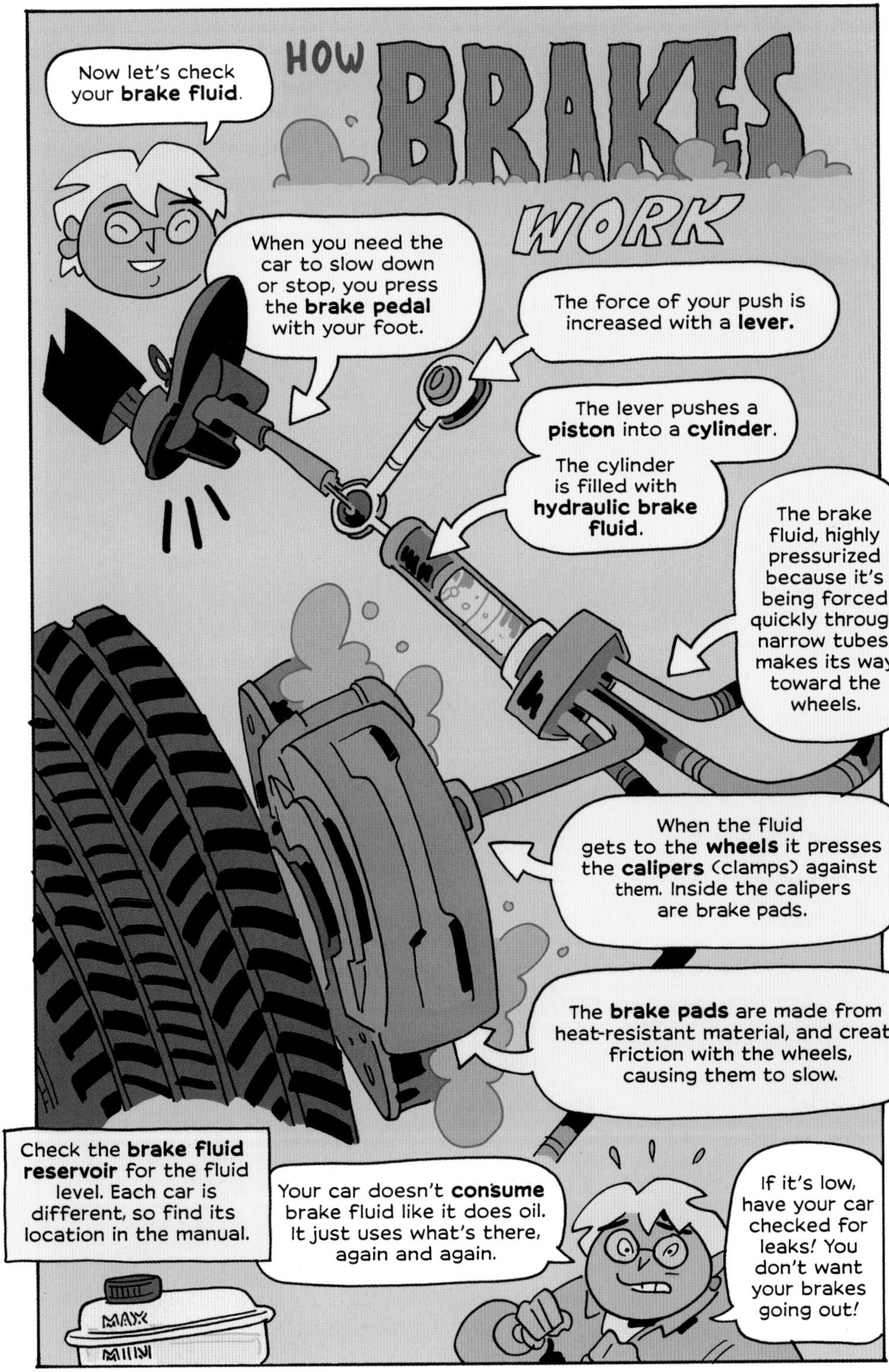

Now let's check your **brake fluid**.
HOW BRAKES WORK
When you need the car to slow down or stop, you press the **brake pedal** with your foot.
The force of your push is increased with a **lever.**
The lever pushes a **piston** into a **cylinder**.
The cylinder is filled with **hydraulic brake fluid**.
The brake fluid, highly pressurized because it's being forced quickly through narrow tubes, makes its way toward the wheels.
When the fluid gets to the **wheels** it presses the **calipers** (clamps) against them. Inside the calipers are brake pads.
The **brake pads** are made from heat-resistant material, and create friction with the wheels, causing them to slow.
Check the **brake fluid reservoir** for the fluid level. Each car is different, so find its location in the manual.
Your car doesn't **consume** brake fluid like it does oil. It just uses what's there, again and again.
If it's low, have your car checked for leaks! You don't want your brakes going out!
MAX
MIN

The next fluid we'll check is the **windshield washer fluid**.

Know how you check it?

Do you just look in the washer fluid reservoir?

That's right!

If you can **see** it, that is.

On this car, it's right out in the open, but sometimes the washer fluid reservoir is hidden away in the wheel well.

If it looks low, fill it up with washer fluid, and if you can't see it, go ahead and fill it up just to be safe.

WASHER FLUID

Unlike motor oil or coolant, you can't hurt your car by overfilling washer fluid.

And it's important to keep your windshield as clean as you're able!

I **do** like my car looking shiny.

That's part of it, for sure.

But if your windshield is dirty, you can't see very well. Especially at night!

If you can't see well, you're much more likely to get into an accident.

Yikes!

Keep your washer reservoir filled, and the wipers can effectively keep your windshield free of grime spots as they appear when you're driving.

The final two fluids we'll be checking aren't accessible on Mason's car, so we'll take a look at Abner's, which is a little older.

I prefer "classic."

Your car's power steering fluid can be found in the power steering fluid reservoir.

Check the manual to see where it is?

Power steering uses hydraulic fluid to amplify the force the driver uses to turn the wheel. When the **steering wheel** is turned, pressure from the hydraulics helps to push the **rack** connected to the **wheels**, turning them without much physical effort from the driver.

The **rotary valve** recognizes that the steering wheel is turning and opens a channel for the power steering fluid.

steering wheel

Many power steering fluid reservoirs have a small dipstick built into the cap.*

Wipe it, reinsert it, and check the level!

Fluid lines transport the pressurized fluid into a cylinder, pushing a piston attached to the rack and allowing the rack to turn the tires with ease.

The **steering column** controls the **pinion**, a small gear that moves the rack.

The **pump**, powered by an engine belt, provides the pressure for the fluid, but it runs constantly. So to use less energy, many manufacturers are switching to electric power steering, which uses no fluid.

The **rack** is the companion gear to the pinion, a straight series of gear teeth that moves left and right to make the **tie-rods** push or pull the **tires,** causing the car to turn.

* Many other reservoirs are made of partially clear plastic so that you can see the fluid level just by looking at them!

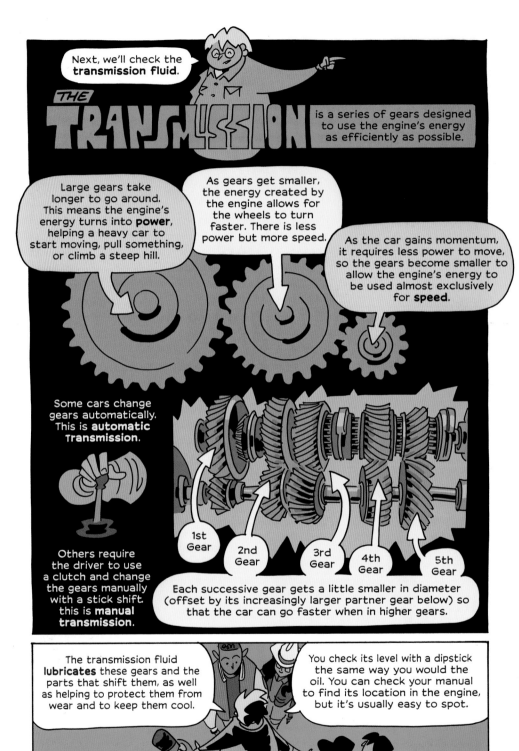

Next, we'll check the **transmission fluid**.

THE TRANSMISSION

is a series of gears designed to use the engine's energy as efficiently as possible.

Large gears take longer to go around. This means the engine's energy turns into **power**, helping a heavy car to start moving, pull something, or climb a steep hill.

As gears get smaller, the energy created by the engine allows for the wheels to turn faster. There is less power but more speed.

As the car gains momentum, it requires less power to move, so the gears become smaller to allow the engine's energy to be used almost exclusively for **speed**.

Some cars change gears automatically. This is **automatic transmission.**

Others require the driver to use a clutch and change the gears manually with a stick shift. this is **manual transmission.**

1st Gear

2nd Gear

3rd Gear

4th Gear

5th Gear

Each successive gear gets a little smaller in diameter (offset by its increasingly larger partner gear below) so that the car can go faster when in higher gears.

The transmission fluid **lubricates** these gears and the parts that shift them, as well as helping to protect them from wear and to keep them cool.

You check its level with a dipstick the same way you would the oil. You can check your manual to find its location in the engine, but it's usually easy to spot.

Your oil dipstick ends in a ring, but your transmission dipstick?

It might have a flat grip.

Your car needs to be cool to check **most** of your fluids, but your transmission fluid level reads best when the engine is warmed up and running.

(Some transmission dipsticks have a "cold" and "hot" read marking, allowing you to check the fluid level when it's not running, too.)

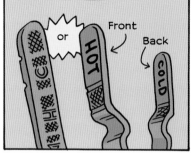

or   Front   Back

HOT   COLD

Abner, turn your car on and let it run for a minute.

You got it, Ms. Gritt!

VRMM

So why can't you check the transmission level on **my** car?

Car manufacturers argue that only **professionals** should mess around with the transmission system.

Most new cars use transmission fluid created specifically for that engine. If a customer or shop puts in another fluid, it might damage the transmission, and if the car is still under warranty, then the manufacturer has to cover the expensive repair costs.

Transmission fluid will easily last throughout most warranty periods, so making it difficult or impossible for the driver to add to it saves the manufacturer money.

But what happens **after** that warranty period? The transmission fluid will need to be changed eventually, right?

Yes, but **you** won't be able to easily diagnose whether or not your car's transmission fluid needs changing. You'll need to rely on a trusted mechanic.

Let's check yours, Abner.

Wipe the dipstick* and reinsert it to get a read.

Even if your transmission fluid is at the "full" mark, check its color. If it's kind of red, you're good; if it looks burnt or brown or black, it's probably time to change it.

Still good   Change

*Paper towels can shed lint and dust, and these can contaminate your car's oil. Use a cloth!

Keeping an eye on your car is **important**.

When your car is running smoothly, it's easy to forget about maintaining it.

But by the time your car starts to **show** problems, it's usually **after** the problem has become bad enough to affect a system.

Those problems can be very expensive and time-consuming to fix. But if you're **vigilant** about your car's upkeep, you can avoid many of those problems altogether!

This doesn't mean that you have to check the fluids every time that you get in the car! If you're not experiencing problems driving, you can check most of them just a couple of times a year.

I recommend when summer starts and when winter starts.

The exception is your **motor oil**. Since your car burns away the oil, it gets used up more quickly than the other fluids.

If you **want** to really stay on top of things, checking your oil level every couple of weeks is a good plan.

So as long as we keep an eye on our fluid levels, we should be able to avoid most preventable problems with our engine?

It'll help, but keeping your fluids in good order is only **one** part of preventive maintenance.

You also want to make sure that the engine itself is up to snuff.

You should examine the more fragile parts of your engine once a month (and before any long trip).

Taking a few minutes to give your engine a good once-over will help you keep your car running well for a long, long time.

Let's start with the **battery**!

BATTERY

Inside your engine are cylinders in which your car's fuel is burned, becoming the energy that moves your car. That same energy keeps the pistons in those cylinders pumping, burning more fuel. But where does the energy come from that gets those pistons pumping in the first place?

It comes from the **battery**!

Positive terminal (red)

Negative terminal (black)

(or occasionally blue!)

The battery's number one job is to start the engine. Once the engine has started, it uses the fuel to supply the power necessary to move the car.* The engine then uses the alternator to recharge the battery as it runs, preparing it for the next time it has to start the car.

There are a lot of places where your battery can show wear and tear.

✳ HYBRID & ELECTRIC VEHICLES

Hybrid cars use a battery to power the car itself, **teaming up** with the engine's fuel to help the car run as efficiently as possible.

When the car first accelerates or drives at low speeds, the **battery** powers the car. As it speeds up, the **fuel** provides the power!

And just like a standard car battery, it is recharged by the engine itself when the fuel begins to power that engine.

Electric cars are powered **entirely** by batteries. Those batteries can be recharged by plugging them into an electric power supply.

Your car's battery is filled with **sulfuric acid**, and sometimes that acid and its vapors leak out, creating powdery deposits around the the battery's terminal.

Deposits

Left unchecked, these deposits can grow rapidly, causing the contact between the battery and the electrical system to fail.

Really bad deposits

These deposits are easy to clean away. But they're very toxic! You don't want to get them on your skin, and you definitely don't want to inhale them or get them in your eyes.

Wear gloves and safety goggles!

And don't wipe your hands on your clothes if you don't want to stain them forever.

Before you try to clean a crusty battery, it's important to disconnect it so that you don't accidentally shock yourself or the car's computer or electrical systems. We disconnect the battery by removing **both** of its cables.

Make sure to remove the grounded* cable first!

Both cables are needed to complete the electrical circuit. Without the positive cable, the open circuit will try to close itself. Since the negative cable is grounded to the car, that makes the whole car a part of the open circuit. Accidentally touch the car or battery with a tool, and you could create sparks, or even...

...a violent, acid-spewing EXPLOSION!

*If your car is less than fifty years old, the grounded cable will be the negative cable.

So make sure to remove the negative cable **first**, okay?

. . .

Okay.

Take off the nuts (even if they're crusted over, you can still wipe away the deposit enough to get them loose) and wiggle the cable clamps free.

Make sure the cables are out of the way (I tie them back with zip ties) so that they don't accidentally touch the terminals while you're working.

Mix baking soda and water into a paste, and dunk an old toothbrush in it.

The mix, with a little work from the brush, will clean the deposits away easily!

There are other signs of wear to watch for in your battery, too.

Dropping a heavy tool on it, a car accident, or even extremely cold weather can crack the battery case, so watch for cracks!

Also, keep an eye peeled for frayed or damaged battery cables.

Checking **all** of your cables for fraying is smart, actually.

It's easy for wires and cables to get damaged, so be vigilant!

Checking your hoses for holes and loose connections is just as important.

You also want to check your **drive belts**.

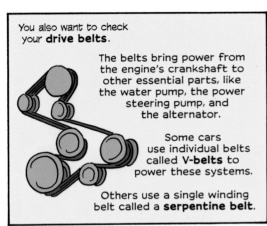

The belts bring power from the engine's crankshaft to other essential parts, like the water pump, the power steering pump, and the alternator.

Some cars use individual belts called **V-belts** to power these systems.

Others use a single winding belt called a **serpentine belt**.

These belts are made of rubber, and they can decay and crack over time. A cracked belt can break while you're driving, leaving your engine unable to function.

It's also a good idea to check your tires.

Do any of you know the **penny test**?

I do!

Yeah, me, too.

Your tire treads wear away over time. If your treads are too low, your tire could blow out.

You're going 70 when that happens?

SCREEE KERASH!

Not necessarily. You still ought to check your treads, though.*

You take a **penny**, turn it upside down, and stick it into the shallowest part of the tread.

If the hair on the top of Honest Abe's head is visible, consider getting new tires. If not, your treads are good.

Good tread!

That's it exactly, Esther!

But if you can't find a penny, you can get a **tread depth gauge** for pretty cheap at a tire or auto parts store.

*Make sure your tires are at their proper pressure to ensure that a tread test is accurate! We'll check tire pressure on page 68.

Also look on the sides for bulges or gouges that can come from scraping curbs.

Between checking your fluid levels and giving your car a quick visual inspection like this every couple of weeks, you can **catch** problems before they **become** problems!

SLAM

We've just got one last thing to check.

My rims?

My tint?

Spoiler? Speakers? My ride's got a **lot** to check, Ms. Gritt.

Windshield wipers!

Oh.

And yours need to be changed, Abner.

See how the end is split and separated? That and the rubber becoming brittle with age will keep your wiper blades from clearing away water properly.

Your windshield wiper blades usually need to be changed once or twice a year.

Changing Abner's will be our **first project**!

I've got some spare blades in the garage!

Me, **I** was kind of hoping we'd do **racing stripes**.

CHANGING YOUR WINDSHIELD WIPER BLADES

Make sure you know what size wiper blades to use. Your manual will tell you, or you can measure your old blades yourself!

It's not uncommon for the driver and passenger side blades to be two different sizes, so checking **is** important.

When you have your new blades, pull the old wipers away from the windshield.

Most will stay out on their own, but if yours won't, fold a towel and put it underneath the old blade so that the spring-mounted arm won't scratch or chip the windshield when you detach the blade.

Different cars use different mechanisms to attach the blades to the wiper arms.

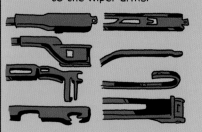

Each of these mechanisms operates differently, so look for buttons or levers to press or pull to disconnect your blade.

When you've released the catch, pull the old blade out. You might have to wiggle it a little if it's been on for a while!

Slide the new wiper in and make sure that it clicks into place.

Once you gently lay the wiper back against the windshield, you repeat the process with the other wiper.

Full wiper blades are made to be changed by customers, but you **can** purchase just the rubber parts.

They're a lot more work to get on, though. Sometimes auto part stores will install them for free, so that can be a cost-effective way to go.

All right, Ms. Gritt. What next?

Well, we've been at this for a while, and we've covered all the stuff I was hoping to get to today.

We'll call it quits for today, but I've got an assignment for you.

Get out your car's manual. If yours is missing, find it online.

I want you to find **all** of the engine parts that we talked about during today's club.

Get to know your car's guts! Point to those parts and say their names out loud.

This will help you to remember them, and you'll know where to look when you need to examine a part.

Now get out of here! Go do teenagey stuff.

Thanks so much, Ms. G.

We'll see you at school!

And next Saturday.

Wear clothes you don't mind ruining!

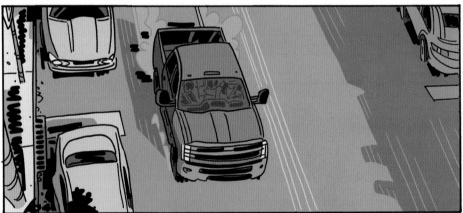

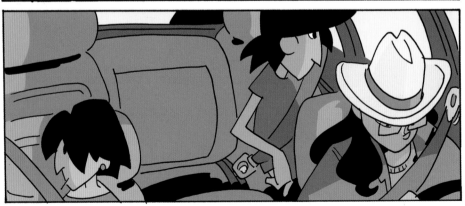

Thanks, Lena.

It's no big deal, Esther.

I passed you last Saturday, so you're on my way.

I'd have given y'all a ride **then** if I'd known you.

I thought I knew **everybody**, but I guess it's easy to miss a freshman or two when you don't share classes.

You didn't miss us.

We're not freshmen.

We're in seventh grade, so we're still at the middle school.

Huh.

Do you know Ms. Gritt or something?

Not really. You know Otto's Auto?

I know where it is.

Otto lets us hang out there sometimes.

He was friends with our dad.

We were there when Ms. Gritt was picking up some jack stands.

She was talking to Otto about Car Club, and we asked her if we could come.

So...

You're not old enough to drive yet.

Not legally.

So what are you getting out of the class?

What do you mean, "get out of it"?

If Ms. Gritt isn't your teacher, then Car Club doesn't give you extra credit for physics.

And you're not fixing a car or anything.

Not being old enough to drive doesn't mean you can't fix cars.

Yeah, we just **like cars**. We like knowing how they work and how to take care of them and how to fix stuff.

I get that.

Me, I don't know squat about how trucks **work**, but I **love** driving. Figure if I'm going to be serious about it, I ought to know at least a little about **what** I'm driving.

It **is** a nice truck. What's it got, a 6.0?

Couldn't tell you, Rocky.

That's why I'm **here!**

Hi, Lena. Go ahead and pull all the way up to the garage, all right?

32

So what are we doing today, Ms. Gritt?

Today?

Today we're going to **change our oil**!

And we're going to do it...

...on Lena's truck.

!

Why Lena's?

I mean, you're fronting the costs for the supplies for these lessons, and we really appreciate that, Ms. G. But I'm just curious as to whether you've got a rotation in mind or something.

My car, Lena's truck, Mason's car, repeat?

That's a fair way to go about it, sure.

But there's a more **practical** reason for using Lena's truck for our oil change.

The truck is **lifted**.

That means it has been raised up higher than when it was manufactured.

I like to go mudding.

When a car or truck has been lifted, it gives the driver the option to add larger tires that raise the vehicle.

This truck has been lifted by adding extra **leaves**. A leaf is a flat type of spring.

The truck is high enough off the ground that we can comfortably get underneath it.

An oil change requires getting underneath the vehicle, so Lena's will be easiest.

If we were to be working on one of the other cars, we'd have to use **jack stands**.

Your jack can lift your car up, but aside from changing a tire, you should **never** do work on a car supported by an automotive jack.

I don't give two hoots about proper automotive safety

CRUNCH

Oh no, now I am dead

Why do I get the feeling that when you describe terrible things happening, you're using **me** as an example?

Jack stands are tools that keep a jacked vehicle **safely** off the ground.

Ratchet style

Screw style

Pin style

But even though jack stands are safe when used correctly, **I** don't feel comfortable having you youngsters underneath **two tons** of propped-up **metal**.

Lena's truck it is.

Lena, how long have you been driving today?

About ten, maybe fifteen minutes.

Perfect. The oil has had time to warm up but hasn't gotten **hot** yet.

We'll give the engine a few more minutes to cool down.

While we're waiting, let's look at the tools we'll be using today.

TOOLS FOR CHANGING OIL

OIL FILTER WRENCH
to remove the oil filter

OIL DRAIN PAN
to catch the old oil for recycling

COMBINATION WRENCH
to remove the oil pan's drain plug (check manual for size: probably a 15mm, a 13mm, or a standard 7mm)

OIL
to refill your engine's oil pan (check the manual to know which type you should use)

LATEX OR RUBBER GLOVES
to keep your hands clean

OIL FILTER
to replace the old oil filter (check the manual for this one, too)

Now, the first thing we're going to do is reach into the engine and remove the oil cap.

When you release liquid from a container, air needs to rush in to fill the empty space.

That's why a big bottle of soda will "glug, glug, glug" if you try to pour it all out at once. The soda has to give the outside air its "turn" to go in as the soda goes out.

GLUG G GLUG

If a container has an extra hole into which air can rush as the liquid leaves, then there's no glugging.

Removing the oil cap creates that hole, letting air in when we start to drain the oil below. This makes for a smoother drain and less of a mess!

All right! Let's get underneath this beast.

Can anybody tell me where the oil pan is?

Is this it?

Nope. Good guess, though.

That's the transmission pan.

The oil pan will be under the engine itself, nearer the front.

I don't see it.

This one's tricky. It's got a splash shield, which protects the engine from road debris but makes underside access trickier.

Some car maintenance might require removing the shield, but you can get to the oil pan and filter by going around its side.

Make sure you've got your gloves on and that you've got your drain pan or bucket ready to catch the old oil.

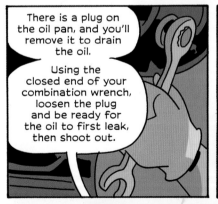

There is a plug on the oil pan, and you'll remove it to drain the oil.

Using the closed end of your combination wrench, loosen the plug and be ready for the oil to first leak, then shoot out.

Keep turning until the plug comes off. Keep your hands clear in case some of the oil is still hot!

Now we give it a few minutes to drain.

Once the oil has all drained out, we'll put the plug back in.

First, though, we're going to replace the gasket.

The **gasket** is a small, round washer that serves as a seal for the plug.

They only cost about a dollar, so it's always worthwhile to use a new one with each oil change.

Gasket

Oil plug

With the new gasket in place, screw the plug back in by hand, then **gently** tighten it with your combination wrench.

Next, we look for the **oil filter**.

An oil filter is about the size of a fat soup can and has a rounded bottom.

As oil moves through the engine, it picks up traces of dirt and rust. It travels into the filter...

...where the contaminants are caught by folded filter fibers. The clean oil travels back through the engine, and the process repeats.

You might be able to unscrew the filter by hand, but if not, use an oil filter wrench.

Avoid using an adjustable wrench. It can crush the filter. **Huge** mess!

Make sure your drain pan is underneath the filter when it comes off. There will be oil in and above it!

All right!

Time to break out the new oil!

Each engine uses a different type of oil. How do you find out which oil your car takes?

"Check the manual."

That's right! Lena's truck uses OW-20.

We're going to pour a teeny bit into our brand-new oil filter. This will help to get the oil pressure back to normal faster than if we left it dry.

Rub just a smidge of oil around the new filter's gasket ring.

This will help the oil can go on smoothly, creating a good seal.

It'll also make removing it during your **next** oil change easier!

Tightly screw the new filter into place by hand.

Oof!

Okay, everybody shimmy on out.

Now that the oil has been emptied and the plug and filter are in place, we can refill the engine with the new, clean oil.

And because I like to avoid messes whenever I can, I'm going to use a funnel.

Different engines require different amounts of oil. Lena's takes six quarts.

"Check the manual."

If you're worried that you have an oil leak, now's the time to look under your car for **drips!***

When you've finished pouring in the new oil, close up the cap.

You're almost done!

"Almost"?

We've still got to clean up the oil.

I did a report on it for Earth Day, back in ninth grade.

You can't just throw it away, and you need to be careful not to spill it.

Used oil has toxic chemicals in it, plus bits of metal. Oil doesn't dissolve in water, so when it rains or when it's hosed away, it ends up getting washed into sewers and drains or into yards or ditches.

It can poison plants and animals, contaminate drinking water, and mess up water treatment plants.

That's right, Abner. So we pour the used oil from the drain tray into something that we can seal...

old auto fluid bottles are good...

and we take it somewhere to be recycled.

*To avoid leaks, tighten the oil pan bolts and replace leak-prone parts like rubber gaskets and seals. You can also use **stop leak** oil additives, which soften rubber and plug leaks.

Look online to find your nearest oil recycling location.

It might be a city or county hazardous waste disposal site, or it might be a nearby auto parts store.

Don't forget to take the old oil filter with the oil!

All right! Now you know how to change your own oil.

Now, you need to be able to decide whether or not it's worthwhile to do so.

What do you mean?

Because you're not paying for the cost of labor, a lot of car maintenance and repair will cost less if you do it yourself.

Oil changes are the **exception**.

When I was young, it saved you a good deal of money to change your own oil, but oil changes have gotten much cheaper over the years.

Depending on the type of oil your engine uses, you might save a lot, but you may only save a dollar or two. If you factor in the cost of a filter wrench and drain pan, it might cost you **more** money to change it yourself!

It's always good to know how to do things yourself, and changing your own oil can be fun, especially if you like working on cars.

But if you're doing it to save money, be sure to add up your costs and compare!

Now, use the hose to wash off any oil that's on your skin. It's toxic, remember!

And Mason, I noticed your car has been **squeaking**, so we'll all look into that **next** week!

41

All right, class...

Dis-missed!

Thank you, sir!

Mason, hold back a sec.

What's up, Teach?

I noticed that you signed up for testing next week.

Yes, sir. Keen on getting that red belt.

In the past, I've always **invited** you to test.

I didn't this time because I want you to take some time to really get comfortable with the new forms.

But I **am** comfortable with them, Mr. Ortiz. I know them backward and forward!

I've seen that you know the **moves**, Mason. And I know that you're spending a lot of time practicing.

But you're getting into the higher ranks. These forms aren't just new combinations of moves that you know. They're new movements, new techniques.

You've got to give your body time to acclimate to them, let them become muscle memory.

You're a gifted and dedicated student, Mason, and I don't want to discourage you.

I couldn't be more proud of how quickly you've picked everything up.

But getting to your black belt isn't the end goal, and I worry that if you fly through your training to get it, you'll miss out on what earning it can give you.

Hey, look who showed up!

It's ten after, hotshot. You gonna keep us waiting all day?

Don't start with me today, Abner.

I just think it's funny that our very own **Mr. Rules** shows up late without calling when just last week he was giving **me** grief about being only **five** minutes late.

I'm late.

I'm sorry.

Drop it.

Good to see you, Mason. Engine still squeaking a little, I hear.

Start that car back up, and let's pop that hood!

*See page 26 for a refresher on drive belts.

That might just mean that you need to adjust the tensioner using a socket wrench (or maybe a breaker bar, since it will be tight), but you might need to replace the tensioner altogether.

The tensioner nut makes the belt tension looser or tighter.

If the noise **doesn't change** when you spray the belt with water, then it's not the belt squeaking but a **pulley**.

The most likely cause of a pulley squeak is that a bearing has gone bad inside the pulley.

If that's happened, you can remove the old pulley and replace it with one from an auto parts store.

But don't think that your bearings are just fine because the squeak changes when you spray the belt!

They could **still** be responsible for the squeaking noise.

This squeak **disappeared** when you sprayed the belt.

It did! But it'll come back. If the squeaking stops when wetted, that means that it's either a problem with the belt itself or with the belt's alignment.

Sorry...

"Alignment"?

Alignment is when a straight line is created when you go from the position of one thing to the position of another.

Your belt goes through a lot of points, and each point has to align with all the others.

If one of those points isn't exactly where it should be, the belt will be **misaligned**. This will put extra pressure on the pulleys and will cause wear to the belt.

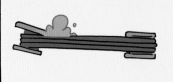

What could make a pulley move out of place?

There could be a couple of different causes for that, Esther.

The pulley might be too deep on the shaft on which it spins, or it might not be on deep enough, to be in line with the other pulleys. This can happen when the pulley is attached to a part that has been replaced.

This is called a **parallel misalignment**.

But you could still have a bearing problem. When a bearing inside a pulley gets worn or broken, it causes the pulley to spin at a slight angle instead of a perfect circle.

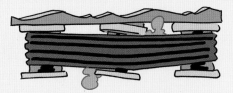

This throws off the alignment and also prematurely wears out the belt. This is called an **angular misalignment**.

Of course, it might not be an alignment issue at all. The belt itself might be worn out.

I don't think that's the case here.

This belt looks brand-new. Not a crack on it!

Then we've narrowed down the problem!

Shut the engine off, Mason. Time to get to work!

Yes, ma'am.

To get to the bottom of this, we're going to remove the serpentine belt.

Any of you youngsters got a penchant for drawing?

Man, Rocky's great. For real. He draws band logos and cars and all sorts of stuff.

I draw **some**, but I'm not an artist or anything.

He's modest. He's really good.

Really **great**. His mom works at my brother's coffee place, and whenever he's there, he's drawing.

Well, I'm **glad** to have a great artist on hand, but don't worry, Rocky. This particular drawing doesn't have to be pretty.

What I want you to do is sketch a little diagram of where the serpentine belt goes.

We'll want to look at it when we put the belt back.

Oh, sure, I can do **that**.

You **could** just snap a photo if you've got a phone with a camera, but I love a good diagram!

So the tensioner? We're going to use our breaker bar to release the tension that it's putting on the belt.

Do you know which way to turn the nut?

You turn stuff left—counterclockwise—to loosen it, right?

Righty tighty, lefty loosey.

Usually, that's correct. But the reason I bring it up now is that sometimes the threads on **tensioners** are **reversed**.

Any guesses on how to find out which way this car's tensioner threads need to be turned?

"Check the manual."

Goodness. Y'all **are** learning!

It doesn't say anything one way or the other.

That usually means that it's the standard counterclockwise-to-loosen threading.

Still, it doesn't hurt to do a quick online search for your car's year and model, and "tensioner thread direction."

Looks like it's regular. Lefty loosey.

Great!

On a newer car like this, you can call a dealership, and they can probably tell you, too.

How goes the diagram, Rocky?

I think it will help us put it back on correctly.

All right. *Woof!* This is tight. Glad we have a breaker bar.

Dad never had a breaker bar, but he had a long pipe that he would slip over the handle of a socket wrench.

It would give him that extra leverage.

Yeah, and **sometimes** he'd come in with busted knuckles when the pipe slid off the ratchet.

There's a reason that specific tools are made for specific jobs, but you can certainly improvise a tool...

especially if you need to do an emergency repair on the road!

Your dad sounds like a clever guy.

There! See, with the tensioner loose, the belt has a lot of give, a lot of slack.

Now that it's loose, you can just slip it off the pulleys.

 With the belt off, we'll use a ruler to check the alignment.

Put the edge of your ruler up against the flat side of any two pulleys. It should be flush with both of them.

Check all the pulleys that way. If one of them doesn't line up, you've found your alignment problem.

They all seem to be straight, best as I can tell.

Okay, so it's not a parallel misalignment. What does that leave?

Angular misalignment.

Which means we need to check the pulleys for worn bearings.

How do we do that?

Give each of those pulleys a little wiggle. They should have a little give, but if you can rock them, that's a sign of a bad bearing.

This one feels kind of wobbly.

That's the **idler pulley**.

So it connects to the idler? What does the idler do?

There isn't an "idler."

It's called an idler pulley because it doesn't directly supply power to a part of the engine like the other pulleys do.

If it doesn't serve a purpose, why is it there at all?

It doesn't power a part, but it **does** serve a purpose.

It supplies tension to the belt and helps to define the belt's path, moving it out of the way of other engine parts.

This one's only got one bolt. Lena, why don't you remove it?

Okay.

Wait, we're taking it off without a new pulley to put in its place?

Figured it was probably a pulley, so I grabbed one of each for this model from Otto. He said I could just bring back the unused ones later, and pay for the one we kept.

Got the bolt off, Ms. Gritt.

Thanks, Lena! Now we can slip the pulley off...

...and check to see if its bearing really has gone bad!

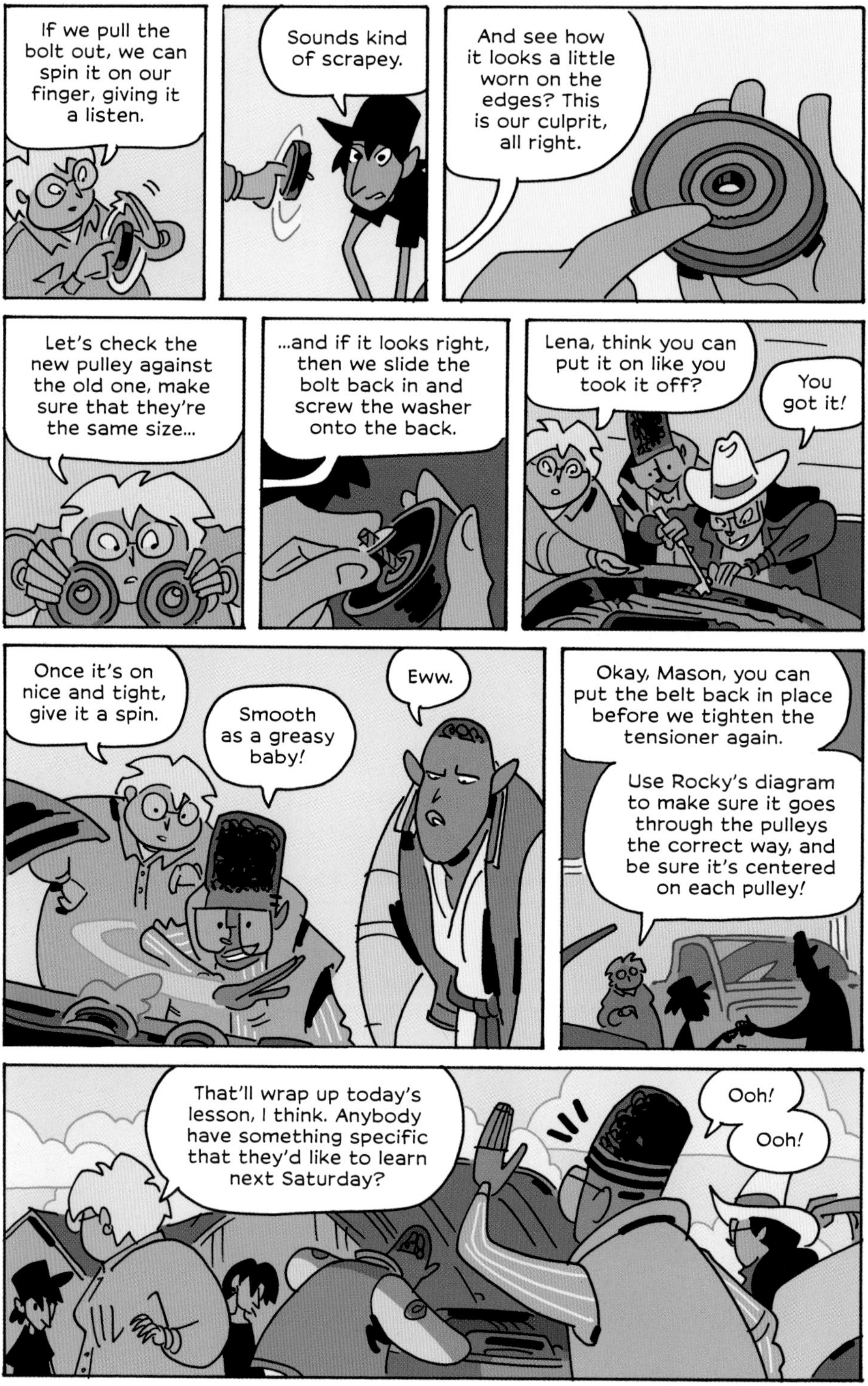
If we pull the bolt out, we can spin it on our finger, giving it a listen.
Sounds kind of scrapey.
And see how it looks a little worn on the edges? This is our culprit, all right.
Let's check the new pulley against the old one, make sure that they're the same size...
...and if it looks right, then we slide the bolt back in and screw the washer onto the back.
Lena, think you can put it on like you took it off?
You got it!
Once it's on nice and tight, give it a spin.
Smooth as a greasy baby!
Eww.
Okay, Mason, you can put the belt back in place before we tighten the tensioner again.
Use Rocky's diagram to make sure it goes through the pulleys the correct way, and be sure it's centered on each pulley!
That'll wrap up today's lesson, I think. Anybody have something specific that they'd like to learn next Saturday?
Ooh!
Ooh!

Detailing! I want to learn how to make my ride sparkle like a chrome-plated diamond in a glitter factory.

...

Okay. We'll see what we can do.

Next week...

weather permitting...

we'll make your cars look as good as we can.

Aw, yeah!

BUT

What do you **mean**, we can't do detailing today?

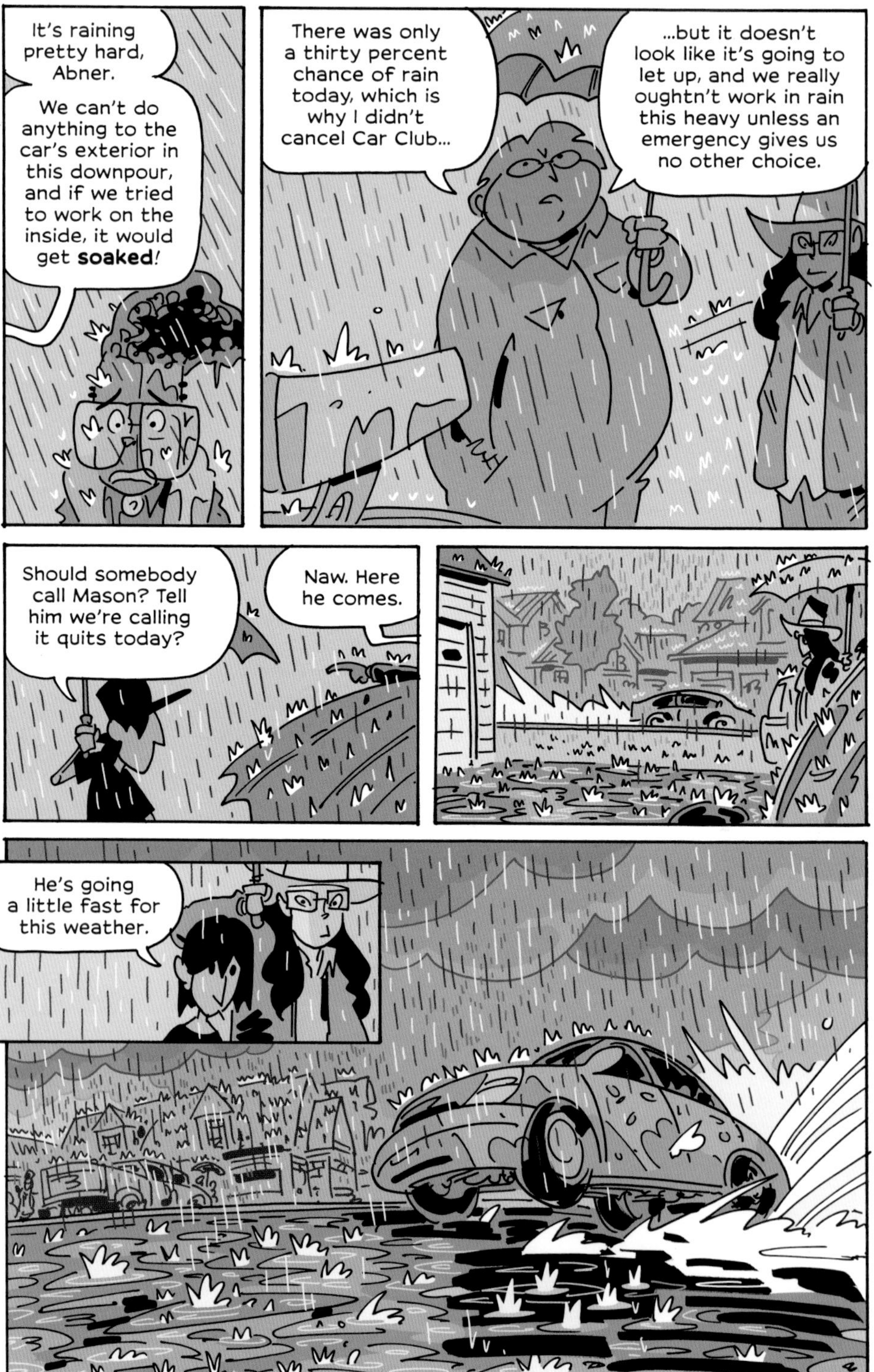
It's raining pretty hard, Abner.
We can't do anything to the car's exterior in this downpour, and if we tried to work on the inside, it would get **soaked**!
There was only a thirty percent chance of rain today, which is why I didn't cancel Car Club...
...but it doesn't look like it's going to let up, and we really oughtn't work in rain this heavy unless an emergency gives us no other choice.
Should somebody call Mason? Tell him we're calling it quits today?
Naw. Here he comes.
He's going a little fast for this weather.

KEERUNCHPOP!

FLAPPFLAPPFLAPP

Um... I think I clipped the curb.

Aw, man. I busted my tire.

You could've done worse than that!

The roads are slick. You shouldn't have been driving so fast!

You're the one who was giving me grief last time about being late! I was going the speed limit.

Yeah, while taking a corner in heavy rain.

What if a **kid** had run out in front of you?

You're like the least responsible driver I know, Abner. I've seen you try to steer with your **feet**.

In an empty parking lot, **not** speeding through a **neighborhood**.

I wasn't speeding!

Gentlemen!

Mason, whether or not you were obeying the speed limit, you **were** going too fast for the road conditions today.

Sorry, Ms. Gritt. I was running a little late, and I kept getting behind slow cars and hitting traffic lights.

We'll get to your tire in a few minutes, Mason.

Let's give our umbrella muscles a rest for the moment, up on the porch.

Woof! It's really coming down, huh?

One of the purposes of Car Club is to make sure that you know how to take care of your car and its parts.

Well, one of those parts is **you**. The driver.

And just like your engine needs fuel and lubrication, **you** need something to make sure you're driving your car the way it ought to be driven.

Tunes?

Time.

When you're in a hurry, you're putting yourself in a position to make bad decisions.

You'll take more risks, because every second that you shave off your trip seems to matter.

Your fellow drivers are part of a **community** of folks whose adherence to the rules and courtesies of the road helps to keep one another safe, but when you're in a **hurry**, they're not your neighbors of the road.

They're **obstacles**.

When you view your fellow drivers through that lens, it makes it easy to ignore that courtesy that helps the roads run smoothly.

And when you drive in a way that other drivers don't expect, the chances for an accident increase dramatically.

Not to mention that when you're sour from your drive, you're likely to **stay** sour when you get to where you're going.

It can be hard to make yourself leave with plenty of time to reach your destination.

Everyone's busy. Everyone's in the middle of something when they know they have to get moving.

But it's **important**. Just as important to the safety of you and your car as brake fluid or working seat belts.

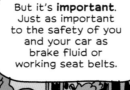

If you know you're going to be late, call whoever you're meeting and let them know. Then drive like you have time.

But that's for occasions when lateness **can't be helped**, and if we're honest with ourselves, we know that most of the time, it can be if we choose to stop what we're doing in order to leave with plenty of time in our pocket.

Being late is like running out of gas. Yeah, it'll happen sometimes, but it shouldn't happen often, and it won't when we're diligent.

I've got a lot on my plate right now, Ms. Gritt.

It's tough to get from one thing to another on time.

I know, Mason. And I know that you're expected to put in the full time at all of your activities.

But talk to whoever's coordinating them. Let them know if you have to leave a few minutes early or arrive a few minutes late.

If none of them are flexible, then you might need to think about which activities are the highest priority and putting the others on hold for the immediate future.

But all of them are important!

I get you.

It's like my class tracks for next year. I can either go the math and science track, or I can go the humanities track.

But that's **hooey.** I like trig and geometry **and** reading and writing stories.

Having to pick one thing over the other is like abandoning half of myself, you know?

Yeah.

Mason's working crazy hard to keep up with baseball, and his classes, and his Eagle Scout project, and who knows what else, right?

A lot.

A lot else.

I'm not giving up writing just because I want to do higher-level math.

Mason shouldn't have to choose between the things **he's** trying to accomplish.

You make a good point, Lena. As you get older, it's tougher to find the energy to try to do everything.

It's easy to forget how important it can be to try.

The rain's a little less heavy, and we don't want Mason's wheel to be damaged by sitting on a flat tire, so why don't we look at this as an opportunity to tackle a new project?

Changing a tire?

Changing a tire.

CHANGING A TIRE

You'll need an **automotive jack**...

My car came with one!

...a **tire iron**...

...and a **spare tire**.

I think there's one with the jack!

Got one of those, too!

Also called a **lug wrench**!

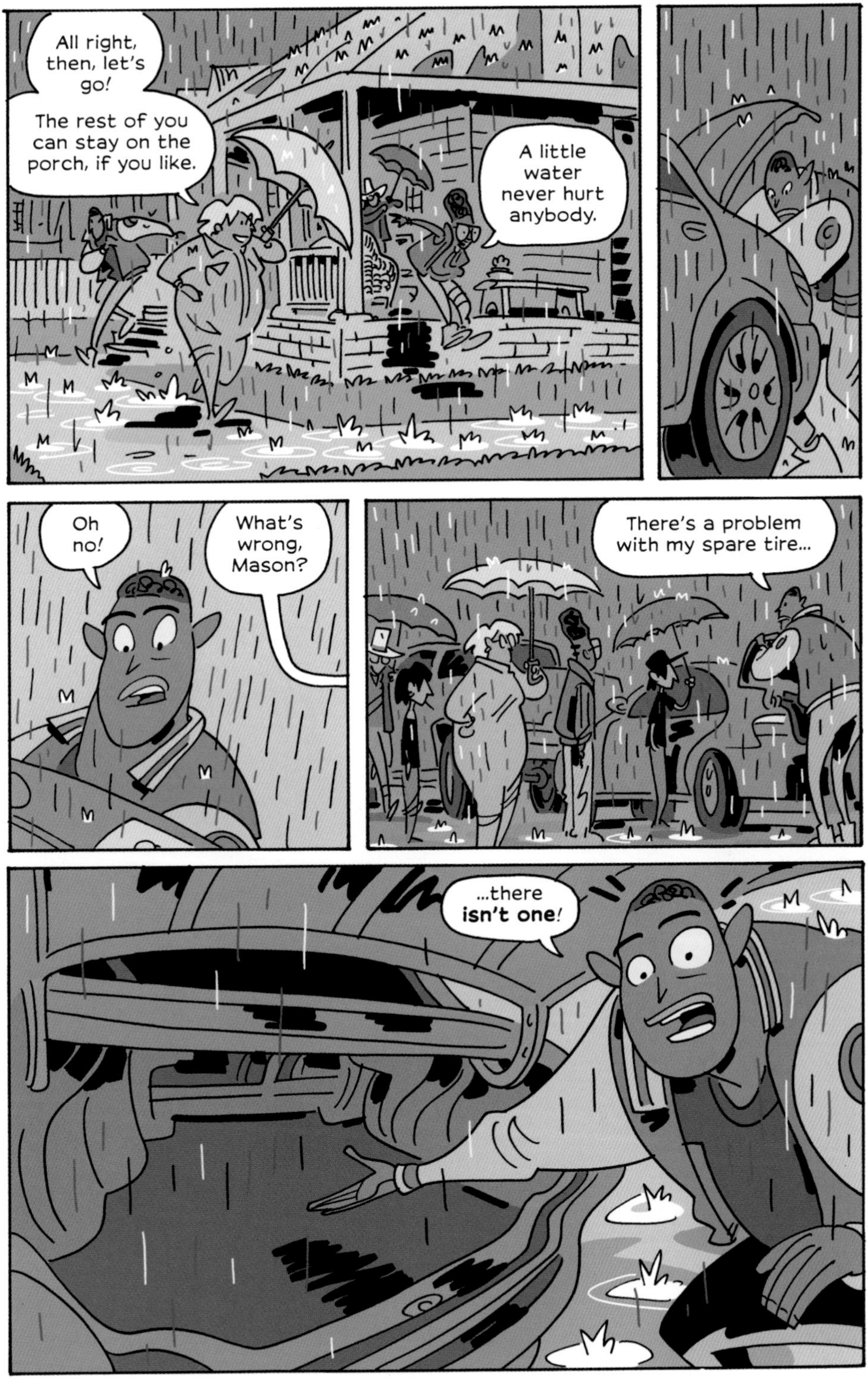
All right, then, let's go!
The rest of you can stay on the porch, if you like.
A little water never hurt anybody.
Oh no!
What's wrong, Mason?
There's a problem with my spare tire...
...there **isn't one**!

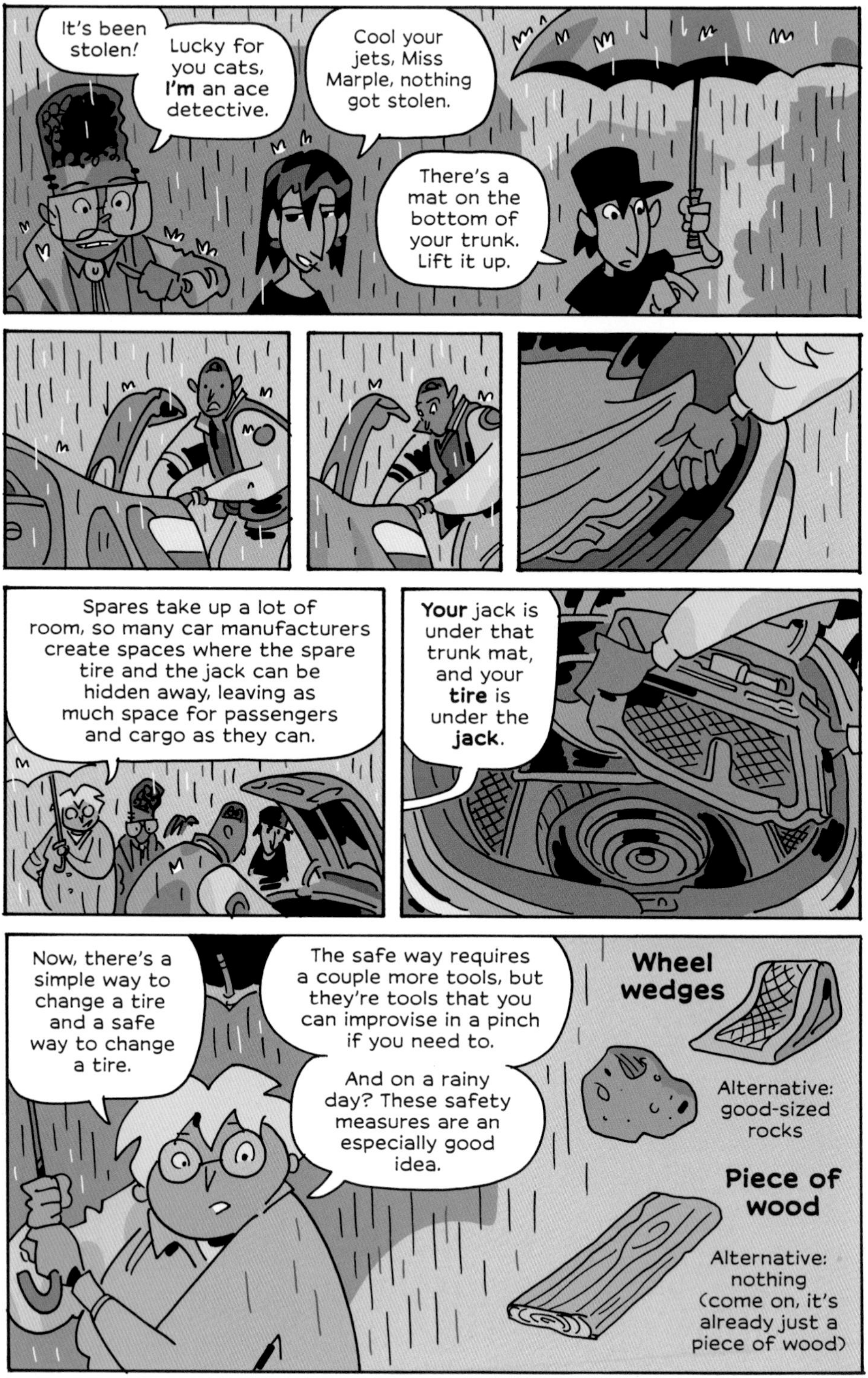
It's been stolen!
Lucky for you cats, **I'm** an ace detective.
Cool your jets, Miss Marple, nothing got stolen.
There's a mat on the bottom of your trunk. Lift it up.
Spares take up a lot of room, so many car manufacturers create spaces where the spare tire and the jack can be hidden away, leaving as much space for passengers and cargo as they can.
Your jack is under that trunk mat, and your **tire** is under the **jack**.
Now, there's a simple way to change a tire and a safe way to change a tire.
The safe way requires a couple more tools, but they're tools that you can improvise in a pinch if you need to.
And on a rainy day? These safety measures are an especially good idea.
Wheel wedges
Alternative: good-sized rocks
Piece of wood
Alternative: nothing (come on, it's already just a piece of wood)

How did you know you had a spare tire but knew not where it was?

I forgot. I've never used it.

Your parking brake is on. Good! That's important.

First thing we're going to do is wedge the wheels so that there's no chance of the car rolling off the jack.

I've never seen anybody do any wheel-wedging when changing a tire.

Most people don't bother, but if you've got the means to do it, you might as well.

Even if you keep yourself safely clear of the vehicle while you're changing the tire... which you **should**...

your car could be badly damaged if it rolled off the jack. Why take the risk?

A pair of wedges, also called wheel chocks, will only run you a few dollars. They're worth keeping with your jack!

If you don't have wedges, use a couple of rocks.

If your back tire is flat, put them against your front tires. If your front tire is flat, put them against the back tires.

And the piece of wood?

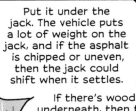

Put it under the jack. The vehicle puts a lot of weight on the jack, and if the asphalt is chipped or uneven, then the jack could shift when it settles.

If there's wood underneath, then the jack will dig into the **wood** as it settles, keeping your car sturdy while it's lifted.

But before we use the jack, we're going to loosen the **lug nuts**!

Before we jack the car up?

Sometimes you really have to give those lug nuts the business.

If your car is jacked up, you might knock it clear off the jack when you use the tire iron to get the lugs off.

If you have a hubcap, it might cover the lug nuts, and you'll need to take it off first.

The lug nuts connect the wheel to the vehicle.

To get them off, you'll put your tire iron over them and turn them counter-clockwise.

Won't budge.

This is why we loosen the lug nuts **before** we jack the car.

Put the tire iron parallel with the ground on the left side of the tire that you're changing...

...and **stomp on it!**

SCREAK

There are more practical means by which to start that nut moving, but nothing as fun as stomping.

Use the tire iron until the bolts can spin easily, then move to the other nuts and do the same.

Don't remove the lug nuts yet!

Now we check the manual to see **where** we should place the jack.

Yours goes **there,** on that bar just behind the axle.

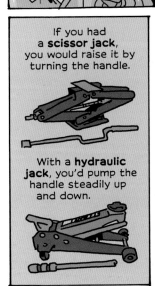

If you had a **scissor jack**, you would raise it by turning the handle.

With a **hydraulic jack**, you'd pump the handle steadily up and down.

Mason, you have a type of **bottle jack**. You **turn** the handle on this one.

Go ahead and get it going. You don't have to position it until it's almost as high as where it will be making contact with the car.

Once it's close, make sure it's squarely on the wood, and line up the top exactly where you want it to make contact.

Now raise the jack until the flat tire comfortably clears the ground.

Now you can remove the lug nuts.

You should be able to unscrew most of them by hand, but the last one will have pressure on it from supporting the entire wheel all by itself, so you'll probably need to use the tire iron.

Carefully pull the tire straight toward you until it's off its lug bolts.

Be gentle so as not to rock the car off the jack.

Set it on its side, so that it doesn't roll away.

Got your spare ready?

I've got it ready.

This is a compact, limited-use tire. Folks call them "donuts."

Donuts serve one purpose: to get you to a place where you can repair your tire or buy a new one.

They're not meant to go fast or far, and many of your car's systems don't work properly with them, so **never** just drive around on a donut.

If you can afford to do so, it's a **really** good idea to replace your donut tire with a **full-size spare**.

You can get the exact same kind of wheel and tire as what your car is already using and store that in the spare tire well.

If the well is made for a donut, there's a chance a full-size tire won't fit, so check.

And if you find yourself getting new tires, that's the perfect opportunity to land a full-size spare.

Just keep whichever of your old tires is in the best shape, and have it mounted on a new spare wheel!

Having a full-size spare is important if you ever take long trips. If you have a full size, you can change your tire and finish your trip, repairing the flat tire when you get back home.

If not, your trip will have to be put on hold while you try to find an open tire repair place and wait to get the flat tire fixed or replaced.

Is the spare on nice and solid?

As solid as it can be without putting the lug nuts back on, I guess.

Well, let's put them back on! To distribute the weight evenly, put each new bolt on across from the last one.

Tighten them with your fingers. Don't use the tire iron yet since it could rock the car.

Once they're all on reasonably snug, lower the jack. With a bottle jack, that means turning the handle again, counterclockwise this time.

Let it go down until the wheel is resting on the ground, but don't take it farther than that. The weight of the car should still be on the jack rather than the tire.

Now that it can't fall off the jack, go ahead and use that tire iron to tighten those lug nuts. Tight as you can, Mason!

That's as tight as I can do it.

Great! Now we lower the jack the rest of the way, and put the flat tire in the spare tire well. Put the jack away, too, and the tire iron.

You can use a tire gauge (a small, cheap tool you should keep in your car) to check the pressure on the spare. Make sure it hasn't lost air while waiting to be used.

It'll say how many pounds of pressure per square inch the tire should be inflated to on the tire itself.

This says "60 PSI."

To check your tire's pressure, unscrew the little air cap and put the open side of the tire gauge tightly against the valve.

The air inside the tire will push a little reader out of the bottom of the tire gauge.

Check that against your tire's specifications, and if it's low, find an air pump at a gas station and fill the tire, checking your gauge as you do so.

Mason, that tire likely isn't repairable. You'll need to get a new one, first thing.

≶sigh≷

I know.

All right, youngsters. Time to get out of the rain. And if it's sunny next Saturday...

"...we'll get your cars shining!"

This here is a **shop vac**.

It's a powerful vacuum cleaner.

It'll suck up all kinds of stuff that a regular vacuum couldn't, wet and dry alike.

If you don't have one, that's okay...

VACUUM

...car washes and some gas stations have coin-operated ones available.

We're going to use this shop vac to clean the inside of your cars.

But that's not all we'll be using!

TOOLS TO MAKE THAT INTERIOR SPARKLE

Cloth

Carpet shampoo

Multi-purpose cleaner

Glass cleaner

Compressed air

Brushes

The first thing we do is make sure that your car is free of junk and trash...

There's probably more of it than you'd expect!

Even if you keep your car free from trash, you might have things like headphones, or a notepad, or spare change, or a pencil, or receipts...

These all have to go!

Throw them out?!

Abner, I'm not going to make you throw out anything that isn't trash.

But we **do** need to get it out of the car.

That's why it's good to have a small bin or a shoebox when you set out to clean your vehicle.

Throw out whatever's trash, and put anything else in the box.

Leave nothing **in** the car that isn't a part **of** the car.

Once that's taken care of, we can start the **cleaning**!

Can we call it "detailing"?

"Cleaning" is boring. I clean stuff all the time. I never get to do **detailing**.

Man, when have **you** ever cleaned something?

Actually, Abner's right!

What we're doing today goes beyond just cleaning.

We **are** detailing!

Let's pull out all the floor mats!

You kids ever beat a rug?

If that's old lady slang for dancing like the stars, you better believe it, Ms. G!

I mean it quite literally in this case, Abner.

Even the **best** vacuum cleaner can't get out dirt and dust the way a good **beating** can!

I use a **tire thumper,** which on larger vehicles with lots of wheels can be used to get a quick sense of whether they're fully inflated by giving them a whack and listening to the sound the tires make.

TIRE THUMPER

But you can use a piece of pipe, or a tennis racket, or just about anything that you can swing.

You can drape your mat over a clothesline, but I don't have one...

...so I hold mine with one hand and whack it with the other!

WHUMPWHUMPWHUMPWHUMP
WHUMPWHUMPWHUMP

Keep at it until no more dust comes off. It may take just a couple of whacks; it may take a couple dozen!

Now, you can't beat the floors themselves, but you can give them a good vacuuming with the shop vac.

Get all around the pedals, and under and between the seats!

If there are stains, spray them with the carpet shampoo. Read the bottle to know how long it should sit.

You don't have to get car-specific shampoo; any carpet shampoo will do.

While your shampoo sits, we'll start cleaning all the nooks and crannies. Now's when you want your brushes!

First, we'll use a little vent-cleaning brush. You can slide one of these in and out of your air vents.

(or you could use a cotton swab)

You can use an old toothbrush to clean inside cracks and crannies, like the inside of a door handle or next to the gearshift.

Use that canned air to blast dust out of console buttons and any cracks or crevices that the brushes can't reach.

Once you've gotten all the spots where dirt and crumbs can hide, you can wipe and scrub away all the debris you kicked up.

Spray or pour a little bit of your multipurpose cleaner onto a rag...

...then use it to clean the dashboard, the steering wheel, the steering column, the console, all that stuff.

If you start to pick up dirt and crumbs and such with the rag, take it outside the car and shake that stuff loose.

Otherwise, you'll just end up spreading it around the car.

Once your shampoo has had the proper time to sit, you can scrub those stains in the carpet up with a rag.

You can hit the deep stains with a scrub brush.

They've got stiff bristles.

The longer a stain sits, the harder it is to get out, which is why doing this every month or so is a good idea.

If scrubbing won't get a stain out, you might want to try a heavy-duty stain remover, but be sure to read the label and make sure that it's okay for use on car interiors.

It's important to clean the windows and windshields, too.

Not just to make it look nice, either!

Why else?

Visibility. If your glass is clean, you can see out of it better.

That's right! A lot of people remember to clean the outside of their windows, like when you wash the car...

...or at a gas station, where they have those squeegee things at the pumps!

Yep! But the outside isn't the **only** part of the windows that needs to be cleaned.

Residue given off by plastic and the grease from your skin and hair can build up on the glass, and that gives dust and grime a foothold.

This can make parts of your windshield and windows murkier than others. You may not notice in daylight...

But at night it can produce **glares** from the headlights and taillights of other cars.

This can make it harder to determine where those other cars are, if there are obstacles in the road, and even where the road itself is. Poor visibility can lead to bad accidents!

Now, regular glass cleaner is fine for most windows and windshields, **unless** they have custom tinting, like Abner's.

Hmm.

Many glass cleaners are ammonia based. The ammonia can break down the tint and cause it to bubble and peel over time.

You can get tint-specific window cleaners at an auto parts store, or you can cut your window cleaner with water, mixing a solution that is about one-fourth cleaner with the rest being water.

If you want to be really crafty and avoid the ammonia altogether, you can make up your own solution with water and a few capfuls each of rubbing alcohol and white vinegar.

Whatever you're using to clean, you won't have to use much to do the job!

When you're cleaning your windows, your best bet is a microfiber cloth.

These cloths have much, much tinier fibers, which means that they can pick up much tinier particles, which the larger fibers of regular cloth might brush right past.

Since much of the residue that builds up on your windows is tiny and slick, microfibers can do a better job than any old rag.

Because the small fibers do a lot of the work themselves, you don't need nearly as much cleaning solution to break down the grime to where the cloth can clear it away.

Just spray a little bit on the cloth itself every few wipes. That way you don't end up overspraying the glass and having to clean up drips.

Do we clean outsides of the windows next?

Nope. We do all the inside before any outside.

Our last step on the inside is to polish the parts that aren't cloth, like the dashboard, the steering wheel, and the seats if they're made of vinyl or leather.

Some people like to use an oil-based protectant on their interiors. These can protect the car's interior to a degree and can make them look rich and shiny if you reapply it regularly.

Shiny!

But oil-based products aren't great for vinyl and plastic, and I don't like the greasiness that sometimes accompanies it.

Doesn't bother me any! Can I have some of that protectant for my dash, Ms. G?

I don't have any here, Abner, but you can pick up a bottle anywhere that sells car stuff.

Also, keep in mind that if your car has leather seats or interior parts, you should apply a leather conditioner after cleaning it.

Otherwise that leather will eventually start to crack!

Once the insides of everyone's cars are clean, we'll move to the outsides.

Make sure that your mats are back inside and vacuumed and that your windows and doors are shut.

WASHING YOUR CAR

SOME TIPS TO KEEP IN MIND

Be prepared to get wet. Don't wear a tuxedo or something, unless you're, like, doing a bit.

Incongruity is **funny**, baby.

Make sure that your car is parked in the shade or that it's a cloudy day. You want to be the one doing the drying. Don't let the sun beat you to it.

Have all your tools on hand and ready to go. You'll need some cloths or towels, a sponge or a washing mitt, a scrub brush, car washing detergent, and a couple of buckets.

Start with the tires. Use a hose to spray away as much dirt, mud, gravel, and grime that may have accumulated on the tires and in the wheel wells.

RAGS

76

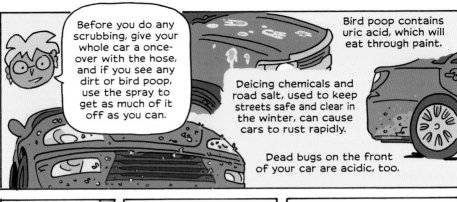

Before you do any scrubbing, give your whole car a once-over with the hose, and if you see any dirt or bird poop, use the spray to get as much of it off as you can.

Bird poop contains uric acid, which will eat through paint.

Deicing chemicals and road salt, used to keep streets safe and clear in the winter, can cause cars to rust rapidly.

Dead bugs on the front of your car are acidic, too.

Now get your buckets full of water.*

One of them should be **just** water...

...and the other should have a little bit of **car-washing detergent** mixed in as you fill it.

Make sure the detergent that you're using is made for cars. Regular soap and cleaning detergent can strip away the wax and clear finish on a car, which will in turn hurt the paint.

Once your buckets are full and the loose dirt has been sprayed clean from the car, focus on the **tires**.

The tires are probably the dirtiest part of your vehicle, and they can pick up bits of grit that can scratch your car if they get on your cleaning rags. Getting all that stuff out of the picture before working on the car's body is the best way to go.

Take a rag and, if needed, a firm-bristled brush, dip them in the detergent water, and get whatever might still be on the tires.

You'll empty and clean the bucket and mix up another batch of detergent water when you're done with the tires. The old water's too dirty!

Get inside all the holes or spokes of your wheels and around the bolts!

Do this for all four wheels, then give it another spray with the hose to clear off any grit that might be left.

*Warm water works best if it's available.

If you notice dirt, grime, or grit on your rag or your brush, rinse it with the hose. You don't want to just smear it around!

Once you've cleaned the wheels...

and getting off the dirt and tar deposits may take more than one wash...

hose them off again.

Now we can wash the car itself. That big bucket of soapy water?

Dip your sponge or your wash mitt in there, and then slather up your whole vehicle.

Starting at the top and stopping at the crease that runs the length of the car at around the middle of the tire, begin lightly scrubbing the car.

Lightly is important! If there is dirt or bird poop or bugs caked on, then you don't want to try to scrub it off the way you would scrub a frying pan.

Any bits of dirtiness that have made it past the spraying and the soaping are probably harder than the paint underneath them. Scrubbing hard to get at them will probably just scratch the car's finish.

Try washing lightly, then wash again, rinsing and re-soaping your sponge or mitt each time. It may take a few times for the soap to work those stubborn parts clear of gunk.

Use the unsoapy water or the hose to rinse each section after you've scrubbed it.

Once the upper part of the car's body is clean, get to work on the bottom part, below that crease. It will dirty up your sponge or mitt something fierce, so save it for last, and don't forget to rinse and re-soap it regularly as you go!

Wet the whole car down again with the hose, so that no one part starts to air-dry.

Why not let it air-dry? We're in the shade. Wouldn't it be easier on the car?

It'll leave little water spots. They'll make the car look dirtier, but they can also eat away at the finish and maybe cause the car to rust.

Go over it all lightly with a dry towel. If your towel gets damp, switch to another towel!

When your car is nice and dry, it's a good idea to wax it. Putting **wax** on your car protects it from harsh sunlight, rain, and the road dirt and bugs that pepper it during a drive.

Wax comes in paste, liquid, or spray!

Think of it as a little bit of armor between the elements and the surface of your vehicle.

Wax

Use less than you think you'll need, putting about a quarter-sized bit on the cloth or foam applicator that comes with the wax.

Too much will make your finish look uneven and gunky, and it'll be harder to remove!

Do small sections at a time and rub the wax onto the surface of the car in small, light circles, leaving an even coat.

The wax container will tell you how long to leave the wax, but you should check for yourself.

Drag your finger across the car's surface.

If it smudges, you need to wait.

If it's clear, it's time to wipe the wax away.

Using a good, clean cloth... preferably a microfiber... make light, circular motions to clean off the excess wax.

What's the point of putting the wax on if we're just taking it right back off?

The wax is still there, stuck to the car, but anything other than what directly touches the surface gets wiped away, so any wax that you lay on thick is just wasted.

That's why you only use a little at a time.

So... **Why** is it important to keep your car clean?

It protects your car from corrosion. If you don't keep it clean, dirt and road salt and stuff could cause it to rust out.

That's right! And speaking of salt, in the winter when the roads are salt treated, it's important to spray out the underside of your car with a hose every week or so. The salt can rust the exhaust system and the springs, and do all kinds of expensive damage that won't only mar the look of your car... it'll keep it from running right!

Same goes for trips to the beach. Rinse that underside!

I know **another** reason to keep your car clean, Ms. G.

Psy-cho-logical!

Care to elaborate, Abner?

Well, if your car looks nice, you want to **keep** it looking nice, right?

So you'll probably drive safer and be more watchful and stuff so that you don't mess it up.

That's a good point, Abner. Tell me, are **you** happy with **your** car? Does wanting to keep it in good shape help you to drive safer?

Man, I l**ove** my ride! I **baby** that thing on the streets.

Would you love it **more** if it had...

...a **racing stripe**?

⸮gasp⸮

a racing stripe

ADDING A RACING STRIPE

You'll need:

Rubber spray paint*
*also called
rubber coating spray*

**Plastic sheeting
or newspapers**

and

**Painter's
tape**

*Make sure this is **removable** rubber coating and **not** rubberized undercoating, which **isn't** removable!

Where on the car would you like your racing stripe, Abner?

That's tough!

There isn't a place on my road baby where a stripe **wouldn't** look grade-A rad.

Down the middle of the hood, I guess.

Okay. You've got some chipped paint on your car, and you only want to try this method on areas where the paint and finish are in good shape.

Luckily, your hood seems to be all right.

Now, we haven't waxed **your** car yet,* but it **is** clean, so we can get to it.

The first thing we do is tape **around** where you want the stripe.

Make sure it's good and straight.

Now, tape your newspaper or plastic sheeting all around everywhere that you don't want painted.

Make sure to cover the windshield, mirrors, grill, everything!

Could there be a little stripe inside the big stripe?

Yeah, we can do that. We'll just put down another piece of tape to mask off the part of the car we want staying its same color.

*Wax protects your car from dirt, grime... and paint! Never paint over a coat of wax, it won't take.

Ooh! *And* can we add like a really cool dragon?

Or a tiger!

Or not. Either way.

We'll just do the stripes today.

Shake up your can really well. Really **shake** that thing, for a full minute, vigorously!

Now, the trick to getting a good-looking stripe—or any design—is to do a few light coats.

Spray the car from about a foot away, in a waving, sweeping motion. You should still be able to see the car's color through the paint. That's okay! That's what you want!

Once your first very light coat of rubber paint is on, you let it dry for about ten minutes.

Should we park in the sun so it will dry quicker?

No! The sun will make your car's body hot, which can make it hard for the paint to set right.

Plus, it'll dry unevenly, with the sunnier parts drying faster.

No, you want to do this sort of thing in the shade or a well-ventilated garage.

Once you've waited ten minutes, shake that can again for another whole minute. I'm not fooling!

If the rubberized spray paint isn't mixed incredibly well, it'll be clumpy and might not peel off as easily!

"Peel off"?

Yep. This paint will peel off when you're tired of it, provided that you do so within about six months of applying it.

You don't necessarily want to give a car...

particularly a car on which all of the doors **match**...

Hey!

a permanent paint accent that may not be to everyone's liking.

It would hurt the car's resale value!

So after that can has gotten its second really good shake, you can apply that second coat.

Again, stay really light on its application and spray it in a loose, sweeping motion.

How many coats of paint should we put on?

At least five.

Though if you went with seven or eight coats, the rubber will be thicker, and peeling it off later will be a lot easier.

Six very light coats of paint later...

Looks like the last coat is dry. Ready to see your stripes in action, Abner?

I've been ready for these stripes since preschool.

Very, very carefully, we're going to peel the tape, pulling straight up. Don't pull it sideways or it might tug on the stripe.

If the tape doesn't come up easily at first and seems like it might pull the paint up, you can make a small cut with a sharp knife or a razor right where the paint and the tape meet.

Peel slowly and deliberately.

And *voilà!*

You've got yourself a racing stripe that you can be proud of.

I've never been more proud of **anything**.

My beautiful, beautiful road baby!

Cheddar corn chowder! My truck hasn't looked this shiny since I got it!

Thanks, Ms. Gritt.

You kids are the ones who did the work.

Got a big outing planned for me and my girl here, and now she's looking finer than a Carolina Bristleback at a 4-H pork pageant!

Where are you headed, Lena?

Mudding.

I can't wait to tell them.

Well, you're gonna.

We agreed: **after** we get it looking less like a useless pile of scrap.

Not fighting you on it doesn't mean I agreed.

I hear Lena's truck. Come on.

SCREECH

Hey, y'all...

...hop on in!

My goodness, Lena! You certainly had an adventure.

Yes, ma'am. I was wondering... did you have anything specific you were wanting to cover today?

Oh no!

She's gonna try to rope us in to washing her truck again!

That's **not** why I'm asking.

When I cleaned the mud off my lights, I realized that one of my **taillights** was out.

I bought a replacement at Otto's but figured we could put it in together.

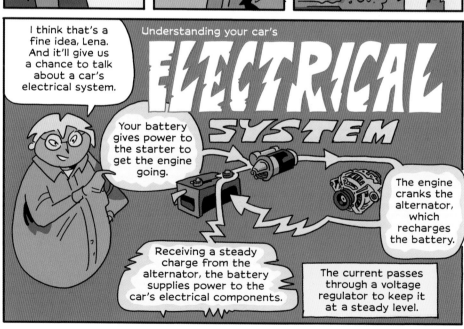

I think that's a fine idea, Lena. And it'll give us a chance to talk about a car's electrical system.

Understanding your car's

ELECTRICAL SYSTEM

Your battery gives power to the starter to get the engine going.

The engine cranks the alternator, which recharges the battery.

Receiving a steady charge from the alternator, the battery supplies power to the car's electrical components.

The current passes through a voltage regulator to keep it at a steady level.

Plenty of stuff in your car is powered by the electrical system.

Windshield wipers

Radio and speakers

Satellite connection for GPS or streaming

Defroster

Power windows and power locks

Plus, it's what you use to car-charge your phone.

And while some radiator fans are driven by the drive belt, others have an electric motor.

And, of course, your electrical system is what powers your headlights, turn signals, taillights, and brake lights.

Turn on your lights and tap your brakes, Lena.

Okay.

Looks like it's the upper light that's out.

Easy enough to replace, if it's just the bulb and not a short in the wiring.

How do you know if it's a wiring problem and not just a dead bulb?

The new bulb won't work.

The taillight covers are held on by bolts. You can access these bolts by opening your trunk or hatchback.

Sometimes they're right there, and sometimes they're hidden behind a panel.

(You might be lucky; some cars have an access hatch behind the taillight that will allow you to change the bulb without removing the bolts!)

On a pickup truck, you'll usually see the bolts when you open the tailgate.

Remove the bolts and then pull free the bulb housing, which is the big colored plastic pieces visible on the back of the vehicle.

Now comes the easy part... getting to the bulb!

Yours has two: an upper and a lower light on either side of the turn signal blinker.

Find the bulb by following the wire.

The wire usually ends at a knob. Twist the knob counter-clockwise...

And voilà! You've got your bulb.

Don't touch the glass part of the new bulb, or the oil from your skin will burn it out more quickly.

Swap it out for the old one and retrace your steps to put everything back how it was when you started.

What about headlights? Is it the same type of thing?

Sometimes, but the newer the car, the more likely that accessing the headlights will be tricky.

Check your manual. Sometimes you'll have to remove engine components to get to them.

My car is like that. But the car parts place swapped mine out **for** me when I bought a new headlight from them. No charge!

A lot of stores will do that. Call ahead and ask.

Now, I'm thinking that we could take a look at that chip in Abner's wind—

Me and Esther got our own car!

Played it **real** cool there, Rock.

You got a **car**! That's great!

We've been saving up, pooling our dough from mowing lawns and stuff.

Bought a derby car off our neighbor for sixty-five bucks.

Plus, we had to pay to get it towed to our place.

But we spent **less** than what we've saved up.

Which is good, because it's going to cost a real chunk to get it up and running.

We **were** going to wait to tell you guys until we had a chance to do some more work on it.

Esther's just embarrassed because it's in real rough shape right now.

Me, I can't wait to show you guys!

If Esther doesn't mind us seeing it before it's up to snuff, you won't **have** to. We could finish out the day looking at your new vehicle.

Okay.

Just so long as you know...

"...it's got a **long** way to go."

It's missing a door!

And a hood, **and** an alternator, **and** some seats, **and** tires, **and** a drive belt, **and** a real fuel tank, **and** brakes, **and** a windshield...

Like I said, it's got a long way to go.

It looks pretty banged up. Was it in an accident?

I wouldn't call it an **accident**.

Our neighbor got it running just enough to enter it in a demolition derby a couple of months back.

What's a demolition derby?

It's like bumper cars, only with **real** cars. Last one that can still move is the winner.

Sounds dangerous.

Our neighbor once jumped off the roof into a plastic wading pool and broke both of his ankles.

"Dangerous" doesn't usually factor into his decision-making.

So did he win?

Not even close. Car died and he couldn't restart it.

It didn't have an alternator. He jumped it before the race, but the battery gave out a couple of minutes in.

Which is good, because otherwise he'd have smashed the front end trying to win. Dead in the mud, he just took a couple of swipes to the side, so the engine is still intact.

Or as intact as it was when he started.

So what are you going to do with it?

Is it, like, for practicing repairs on?

Practicing, nuthin'!

We're going to soup this baby up and cruise it all over!

But it's... it's... it's not even a **car**. It's just a **shell**.

Well, sure.

Right **now**.

This is a great model. Great car.

It just needs a lot of work.

A **lot** of work.

But the shape it's in... That'll take **forever**!

Yep.

But, hey, look at the plus side! If we're taking forever on the car, we're going to know it inside and out.

Besides, we can't drive for almost four more years.

Can't drive **legally**.

Can't drive legally.

Four years is **plenty** of time to get her up and going.

You're in karate, right?

Tae kwon do.

Tae kwon do. So, you know, it's like **that**.

I don't follow.

Like, you're wanting to get your black belt, right?

I want to **earn** it, yeah.

Earn it! That's what I mean. This car is like our **car black belt**, you get me?

We get it to where we **want** it, we know we **earned** it.

If it takes a while to get there, it takes a while to get there.

Like you and your TKD, right? Not like they just give you a black belt; you've got to earn that thing. Takes a while, right?

...

Yeah. Takes a while.

The journey **is** the destination, grasshopper!

Speaking of destinations, we're nearly at **ours**.

Say what now?

Winter break starts a week from Friday.

That means next week is our **last** Car Club.

Well! We'd better make the most out of next week, then, mustn't we?

Is that your new alternator* on the table, Rocky?

Yes, ma'am.

We're putting the radiator back in now...

Neighbor took it out for the derby.

and we're going to change out the alternator when we're done.

If you're game to wait on putting in that alternator 'til next week, I'd be grateful.

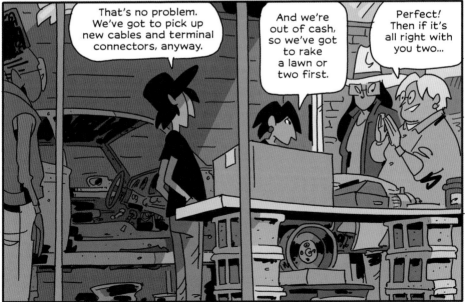

That's no problem. We've got to pick up new cables and terminal connectors, anyway.

And we're out of cash, so we've got to rake a lawn or two first.

Perfect! Then if it's all right with you two...

*The **alternator** uses the running engine to recharge the battery (see page 88)!

"...we'll spend our last meeting on your new car!"

If you're replacing an alternator, the first thing you'd **usually** do is disconnect the battery, for safety.

"Usually" because the twins took the battery out already?

Yep.

So we go straight for the alternator itself.

We'll use a socket wrench to loosen the bolts that connect the alternator to the engine.

Any time you remove bolts, nuts, washers, **anything**, put them all in a spot where you won't lose them or knock them over.*

The serpentine belt is already loose, or we'd loosen it.

The belt runs across the alternator pulley, so you wouldn't be able to remove the alternator if the belt weren't *slack*!

Alternators are connected to the car's electrical system via a wire or wires.

Once the bolts are removed, you can carefully pull the alternator out of its dock to reach and disconnect them.

Then you just **repeat** all of those steps **in reverse** with the new alternator:

Connect the wires, slide the new alternator into place, tighten the bolts, and tighten the belt.

On it!

*You can get a magnetic tray at most auto part stores that's perfect for this job!

And when she's done, I've got the battery. It was charged a couple weeks back, but it's been sitting, so it may need a jump to get it going.

It's not drained, so I figure that the alternator can recharge it if we get it running.

Speaking of batteries, I worked on mine this week.

Worked on it, how?

I noticed it had that blue sandy buildup on the terminals.

So I mixed up a cleaning solution* and cleaned it.

*Page 25!

Were you, like, showing your engine off or something?

Nope.

I was checking my oil and just saw the gunk and figured I'd clean it away.

Abner! I'm so proud of you.

You are? How come?

Checking your oil? Cleaning your battery connections?

Thus far, your only concern for your car has been for its **appearance**.

Well, yeah...

...but that was back when its appearance wasn't **perfect**.

Well, I'm glad to hear that you're giving your car's engine its proper attention.

I've got the new alternator in. It's plugged, the bolts are tightened, and I'm ready to fix the tension on the belt.

Wonderful! Can you reach the tensioner?

No problem, from under the car.

I'll go ahead and put the battery into the battery tray.

Most trays will have some way to hold the battery in place.

This one's got a bar that goes across it and bolts on either side.

Got it!

Done on my end, too.

Great! Now we can reconnect the battery terminals.

Anyone remember which one needs to go on first?

Oh!

You told us that we should take **off** the grounded terminal first...

so that means we should put **on** the cable that **isn't** grounded first!

That's right. And **which** cable is the **grounded** cable?

The negative one!

The black one!

That's right! And if you can't remember, there's an easy way to tell.

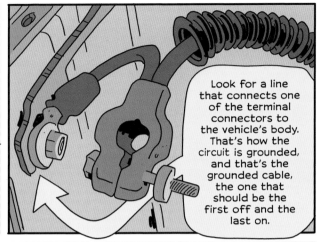

Look for a line that connects one of the terminal connectors to the vehicle's body. That's how the circuit is grounded, and that's the grounded cable, the one that should be the first off and the last on.

These terminals are often made of lead, so be sure to wash your hands **really** well after handling them.

You should wash your hands after doing **any** car work, but lead especially can do real damage to those brains of yours, so you don't want to accidentally touch your lunch or something without getting any traces off your skin.

The positive cable is on. Now I can put on the negative cable.

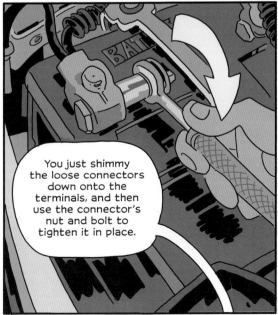

You just shimmy the loose connectors down onto the terminals, and then use the connector's nut and bolt to tighten it in place.

Think we should try to start it?

We might as well try.

Here goes nothing.

CLICK CLICK CLICK CLICK CLICK CLICK

No dice. Won't turn over.

That's great!

I mean, it's not great that the engine won't turn over...

...but it **is** great that we have a chance to use our last meeting of Car Club to go over how to jump-start a car!

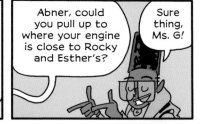

Abner, could you pull up to where your engine is close to Rocky and Esther's?

Sure thing, Ms. G!

Abner, do you have a set of jumper cables in your car?

'Fraid not, Ms. G.

Now **that** is a tool worth keeping in your trunk!

You never know when your car might need a jump to get it home or to a repair shop, and even if you never need it for **yourself**, you'll encounter plenty of **other** people who will.

You may not be in a position to help everyone you encounter, but if you have your own set of jumper cables, you'll at least have the option if you **are** in such a position.

Like a superhero for parking lots!

Okay, first thing's first. Make sure that both cars are off and that they're safely in park.

Or up on cinder blocks.

Does **anyone** here have jumper cables?

I got some, Ms. Gritt.

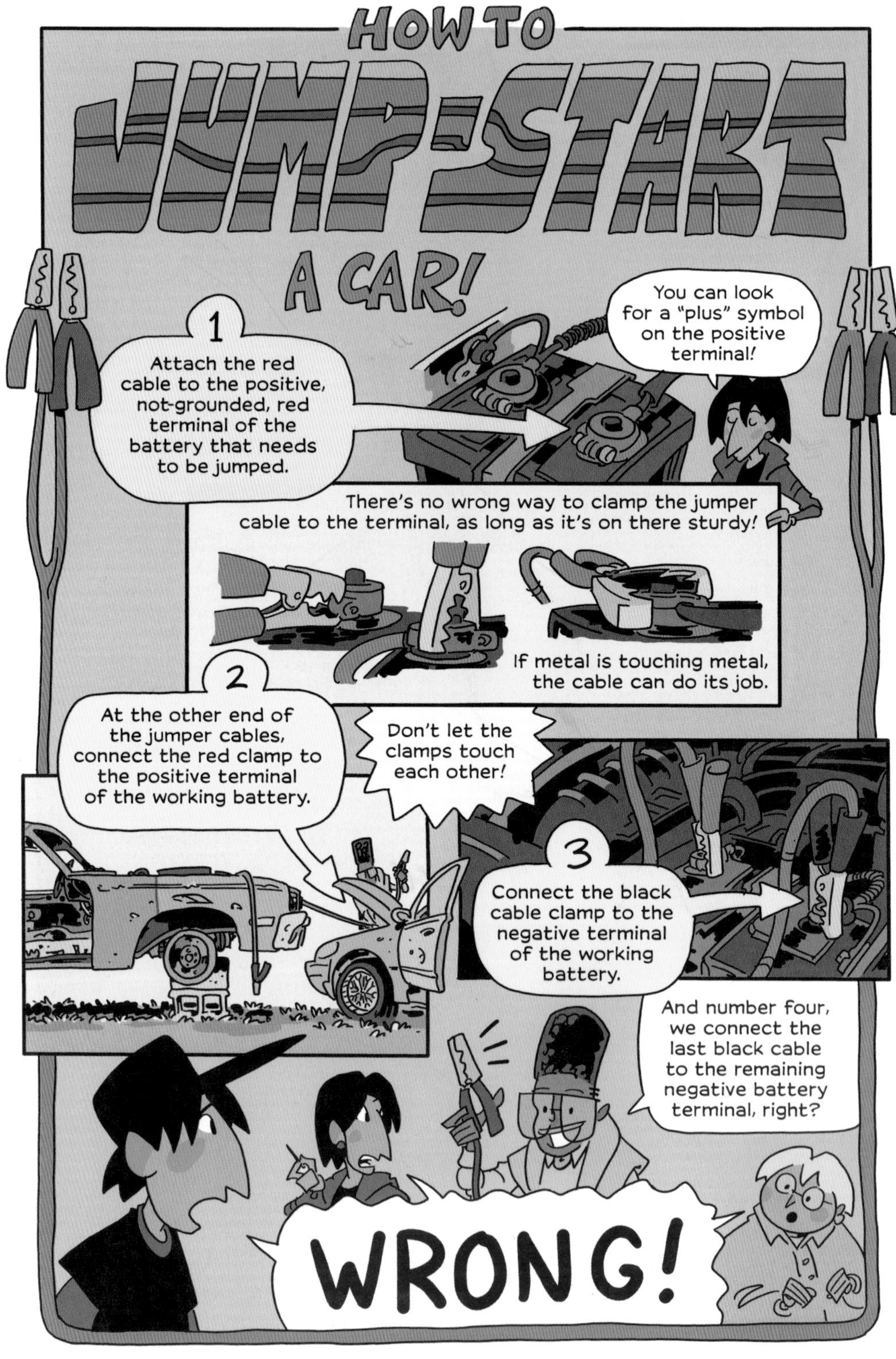

HOW TO
JUMP-START
A CAR!
1
Attach the red cable to the positive, not-grounded, red terminal of the battery that needs to be jumped.
You can look for a "plus" symbol on the positive terminal!
There's no wrong way to clamp the jumper cable to the terminal, as long as it's on there sturdy!
If metal is touching metal, the cable can do its job.
2
At the other end of the jumper cables, connect the red clamp to the positive terminal of the working battery.
Don't let the clamps touch each other!
3
Connect the black cable clamp to the negative terminal of the working battery.
And number four, we connect the last black cable to the remaining negative battery terminal, right?
WRONG!

Huh? But that doesn't make any sense.

You've got four clamps and four terminals. Where do you put the last clamp if you aren't matching it to the terminal?

Well, Abner, we clamp it to **any unpainted metal part** of the car we want to jump, so long as it isn't a **moving** part.

4 Connect the remaining clamp—

We just went over that!

But I still don't understand **why**.

You remember how the negative terminal of the car is connected to the side of the car's body? Grounding it?*

*page 101!

Since the battery is grounded to the car, clamping the negative cable to the car will **still** complete the circuit.

By allowing the return current to pass directly from the car to the cable...

...it doesn't have to take the extra step of flowing back through the battery.

Cutting out that extra step means that the current flow is stronger and steadier.

I heard that if you connect the last clamp to the battery, you could blow up the car!

Well, **if** the battery had a crack in it, its hydrogen could escape...

...**and** applying the clamp directly to the battery terminal **could** produce an otherwise harmless **spark**.

The spark could ignite that escaping hydrogen...

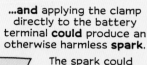

...creating a violent, acid-spewing **explosion**!

Oh no! Dead again!

This is the second time you've mentioned violent, acid-spewing explosions.

Are they, like, **common**?

Oh, good heavens, no!

But mentioning them certainly gets your attention!

No, we clamp the final cable to the car's body for a steadier current, not to prevent violent, acid-spewing explosions.

A cracked or damaged battery is the **real** cause of that kind of danger, so remember to never use a dropped battery or one that is obviously damaged.

Now, the cars are off, but it's very important to make sure that none of the electrical systems are in use.

Headlights

Radio or sound system

Seat warmers

Cabin lights

GPS

Defroster (unless your manual says to have it running during battery jumps)

Windshield wipers

Air conditioner

And make sure to unplug your phone charger!

Right! The jolt from the battery jump can fry a phone's circuits.

5

Turn on the car with the working battery and let it idle for five or ten minutes.

On it!

VROOM

I'm really going to miss working with you guys.

Hey, there's no reason you can't pick Car Club up again after break.

Yeah, there is. Track starts up in January and she's the coach.

My schedule only gives me a window of a few weeks to do Car Club, but I'm sure grateful for those few weeks.

We certainly haven't covered everything, or even a small fraction of everything...

...but what we have covered should give you enough of a foundation to further explore the workings and maintenance of your vehicles.

And even if you don't try to move beyond what we covered, you've still gotten the basic know-how that you need to safely drive and maintain your car.

Well, Abner's car has been giving the twins' car juice long enough to give it a try. See if it'll start.

All right. Take two.

RRRRRRWWRNM

Oh, man. It works! It really works!

Yeah. Yeah, it does!

Great! Now we disconnect the jumper cables, reversing the order of how we attached them.

Making sure the clamps don't touch each other, and taking off the one attached to the unpainted metal first.

Feel that shaking? That's really rough for an idling engine.

Started kind of jumpy, too.

You know what we need to replace...

...the spark plugs.

All right, guys. I've got to go. Thanks again for being a part of Car Club, and I'll see you in school after break!

Bye, Ms. G!

Thanks for doing Car Club!

See you in a couple weeks!

Hey, Esther. Hey, Rocky...

Bye! Thanks!

...those spark plugs, is that something you're going to do today?

No, we'll have to get some. Wires, too.

Probably Thursday, after we get paid for raking leaves.

Think you could wait until Saturday? I'd kind of like to see you go through it.

Yeah, me, too.

"Last week of Car Club," huh?

I'm in if you guys are.

...

Sure.

That would be pretty cool.

Guess Car Club lives on, huh?

Now, if somebody can hand me the ratchet, I can show you something really neat...

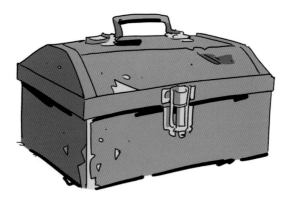

Even though Car Club is over, we have a few pages left in the book.

So let's talk about some of the stuff that we didn't cover.

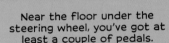

Near the floor under the steering wheel, you've got at least a couple of pedals.

On the left* is the **brake pedal**, We talked about brakes on page 17.

But on the right is the **acceleration pedal**, also called the **gas pedal** or the **accelerator**.

The gas pedal doesn't actually control the **gas**. What it does control is the **throttle valve**.

When you press the gas pedal, it makes the throttle valve open. The harder you press the pedal, the wider the valve opens.

Remember how your engine's pistons are put into motion by lots of tiny explosions (page 15)? Well, explosions are just sudden bursts of energy, in this case fire.

Fire needs two things to burn: **air** and **fuel**.

The throttle valve is the opening through which you give the engine air. Push the pedal down, and air rushes in to make that burn possible.

Brake

Gas

*If you've got a manual transmission, the brake pedal will be in the middle, and on the left, you'll have the clutch pedal.

Clutch   Brake   Gas

(Look back on page 20 for a refresher on how the transmission works.)

The clutch pedal discontinues power to the transmission gears.

When it is pressed, the gears can be switched using a stick shift.

Because no power flows through the gears when the clutch is in, pressing the gas pedal won't result in acceleration until the clutch is released.

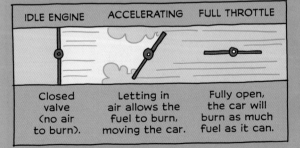

IDLE ENGINE	ACCELERATING	FULL THROTTLE
Closed valve (no air to burn).	Letting in air allows the fuel to burn, moving the car.	Fully open, the car will burn as much fuel as it can.

If your car was made in the last fifty years or so, it has electronic sensors or a computer that measures how much air you're letting in, and it increases the rate that the fuel (gasoline or diesel) flows in to match.

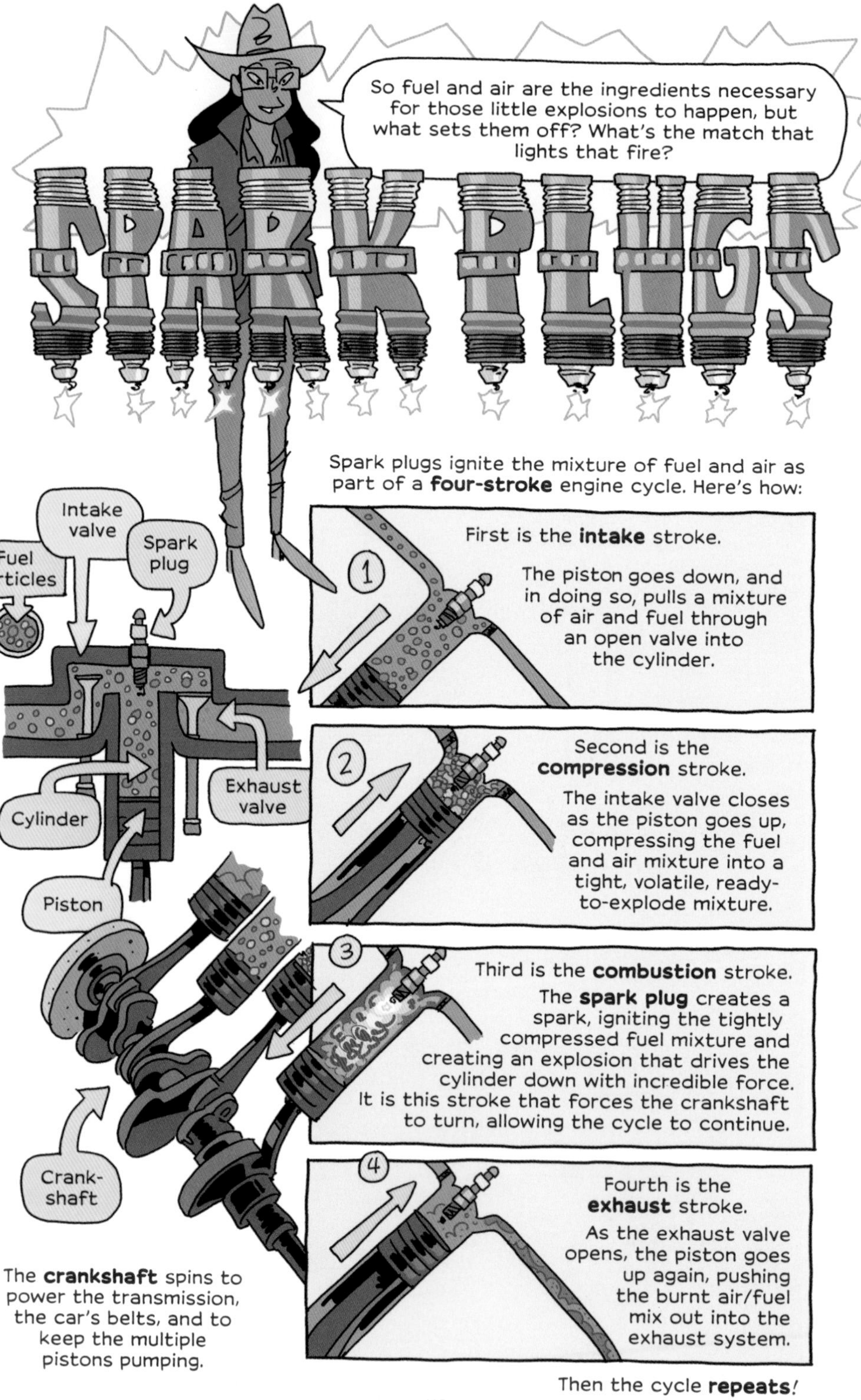
So fuel and air are the ingredients necessary for those little explosions to happen, but what sets them off? What's the match that lights that fire?
SPARK PLUGS
Spark plugs ignite the mixture of fuel and air as part of a **four-stroke** engine cycle. Here's how:
Intake valve
Spark plug
Fuel particles
Exhaust valve
Cylinder
Piston
Crank-shaft
1
First is the **intake** stroke.
The piston goes down, and in doing so, pulls a mixture of air and fuel through an open valve into the cylinder.
2
Second is the **compression** stroke.
The intake valve closes as the piston goes up, compressing the fuel and air mixture into a tight, volatile, ready-to-explode mixture.
3
Third is the **combustion** stroke.
The **spark plug** creates a spark, igniting the tightly compressed fuel mixture and creating an explosion that drives the cylinder down with incredible force. It is this stroke that forces the crankshaft to turn, allowing the cycle to continue.
4
Fourth is the **exhaust** stroke.
As the exhaust valve opens, the piston goes up again, pushing the burnt air/fuel mix out into the exhaust system.
The **crankshaft** spins to power the transmission, the car's belts, and to keep the multiple pistons pumping.
Then the cycle **repeats**!

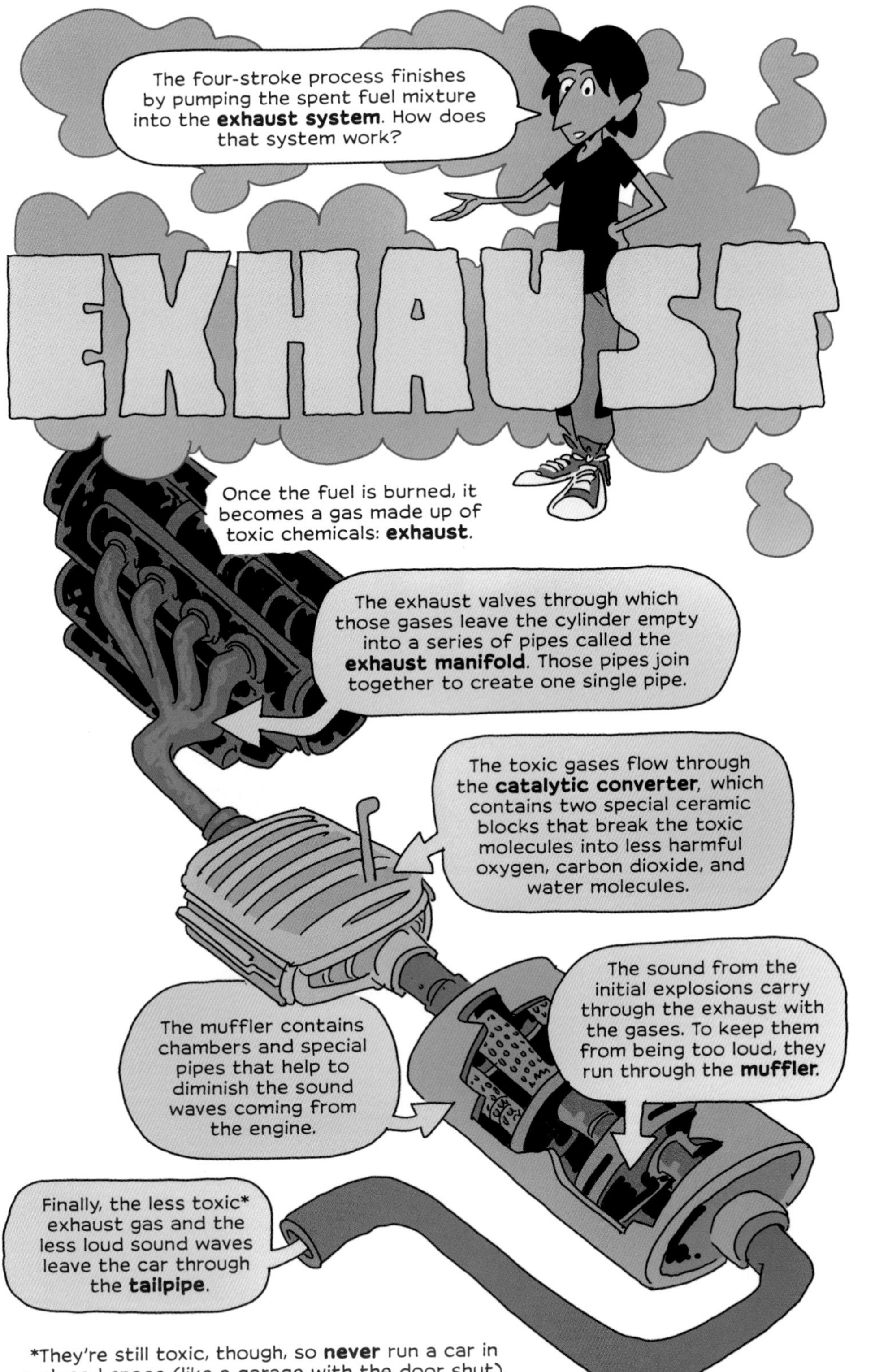
The four-stroke process finishes by pumping the spent fuel mixture into the **exhaust system**. How does that system work?
EXHAUST
Once the fuel is burned, it becomes a gas made up of toxic chemicals: **exhaust**.
The exhaust valves through which those gases leave the cylinder empty into a series of pipes called the **exhaust manifold**. Those pipes join together to create one single pipe.
The toxic gases flow through the **catalytic converter**, which contains two special ceramic blocks that break the toxic molecules into less harmful oxygen, carbon dioxide, and water molecules.
The sound from the initial explosions carry through the exhaust with the gases. To keep them from being too loud, they run through the **muffler**.
The muffler contains chambers and special pipes that help to diminish the sound waves coming from the engine.
Finally, the less toxic* exhaust gas and the less loud sound waves leave the car through the **tailpipe**.

*They're still toxic, though, so **never** run a car in a closed space (like a garage with the door shut).

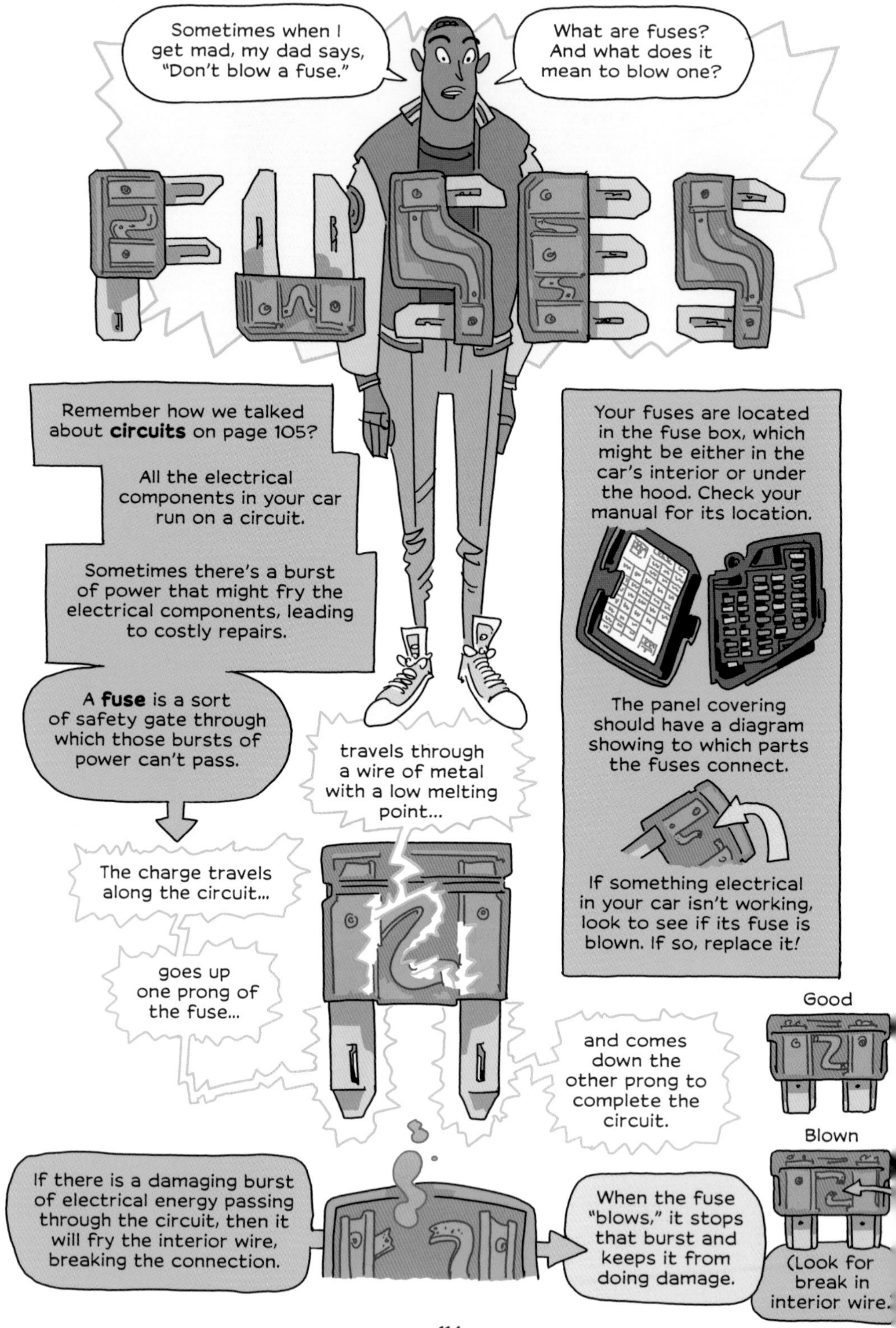

Sometimes when I get mad, my dad says, "Don't blow a fuse."
What are fuses? And what does it mean to blow one?
FUSES
Remember how we talked about **circuits** on page 105?
All the electrical components in your car run on a circuit.
Sometimes there's a burst of power that might fry the electrical components, leading to costly repairs.
A **fuse** is a sort of safety gate through which those bursts of power can't pass.
The charge travels along the circuit...
goes up one prong of the fuse...
travels through a wire of metal with a low melting point...
and comes down the other prong to complete the circuit.
Your fuses are located in the fuse box, which might be either in the car's interior or under the hood. Check your manual for its location.
The panel covering should have a diagram showing to which parts the fuses connect.
If something electrical in your car isn't working, look to see if its fuse is blown. If so, replace it!
Good
Blown
If there is a damaging burst of electrical energy passing through the circuit, then it will fry the interior wire, breaking the connection.
When the fuse "blows," it stops that burst and keeps it from doing damage.
(Look for break in interior wire.)

Your car or truck or SUV is going to hit a lot of bumps when it's out on the road. Or off the road!

But don't worry, your vehicle was designed to take on these bumps using its **suspension** system.

SUSPENSION

When your wheel hits a bump, it goes over it. The wheel is attached to something that will allow it to go up without raising the vehicle.

This "something" might be a coiled spring...

...or a swinging arm...

...or a leaf spring like on Lena's truck (page 33)...

...or other cushioners that serve the same purpose.

But what keeps these cushioners from continuing to bounce after absorbing the impact?

SHOCK ABSORBERS!

Shock absorbers, or **shocks**, are hydraulic tubes filled with oil, located next to or even inside the cushioners.

Inside, there are tiny holes through which the oil flows, and the faster the piston (a rod inside the tube) moves, the slower the oil flows. This helps the shock absorber absorb the different bumps evenly, being more rigid or more loose as the situation demands.

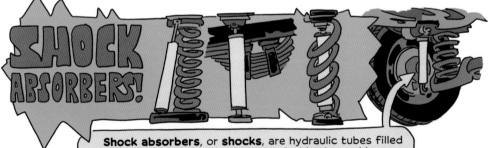

Shocks last a long time, but if your ride is bouncier than you'd like, you might need to replace them.

Push down on your vehicle at each corner. If it bounces up and down after you let go, you probably need new shocks.

While cautious driving and alertness to your surroundings are the best ways to keep yourself and your passengers safe...

...your car has some built-in safety functions that protect you in the event of an accident.

SEAT BELTS & AIRBAGS

When your vehicle is traveling, you're traveling at the same speed. If it collides with something, it stops suddenly... but **you don't**.

Your **seat belt** keeps you from crashing into the dashboard, the steering wheel, or the windshield, all of which could cause serious injury or death.

The seat belt applies the force needed to stop your momentum, spreading that force over a wide, sturdy part of your body to minimize that force.

Seat belt webbing is strong but flexible (at least more flexible than your windshield!).

Usually you can lean forward with your seat belt buckled, thanks to a spooling mechanism called the **retractor**.

But when the car rapidly decelerates or when the belt is jerked, that spool locks in place, keeping you tight (and safe) against your seat.

Even with seat belts, an impact can be very damaging. Another way car manufacturers try to lessen that danger is with the use of **airbags**.

Newer cars are fitted with an impact sensor. If your car hits something, the airbags are deployed to help cushion you.

Airbags have to inflate in the blink of an eye. Fuel inside the inflator is ignited, producing gas to inflate the bag.

The inflated bag puffs up to its full size in time to cushion the impact created by the collision.

The gas almost immediately begins to escape through tiny holes so that you can get out of the car.

An airbag can be a lifesaver, but if you're not wearing your seat belt properly (with its shoulder strap) then an airbag can cause serious injury!

We talked about how your car's heater works on page 15.

But when it's hot out, you don't need a heater.

Luckily, your car has an **air conditioner** for when the temperature outside is making the vehicle's inside uncomfortable.

AIR CONDITIONER

Your car's air-conditioning system is filled with a fluid called **refrigerant**. It changes back and forth from liquid to gas depending on both its temperature and how much pressure it's under.

1
As a **gas** under **low pressure**, the refrigerant goes into the **compressor** where it is compressed into a high-pressure gas.

2
That **high-pressure gas** enters the **condenser**, which works like the radiator,* letting the air from outside cool the refrigerant into a liquid under high pressure.

4
The **liquid** refrigerant, now at **low pressure**, flows through the **evaporator**. Inside it boils into a low-pressure gas again, pulling the heat away from its coils and chilling them with its condensation.

The coldness of the evaporator is blown into the vehicle's cabin through vents, cooling the air inside the car.

3
The **high-pressure liquid** flows through an **expansion valve**, which allows it to expand and lose its pressure.

*See how radiators work on page 15!

117

Well, that's it! I think we've covered all the big stuff, right?

Are you kidding? We haven't talked about the most important thing of all!

SOUND SYSTEMS

Your sound system starts with the head unit. This is the control center of your sound system and is found on your dashboard, usually in the center between the driver and passenger seats.

MUSIC AND STUFF

From here, you can control what plays, the source of the sounds,* and the sound settings. In newer systems you can link your head unit to your phone for hands-free talking.

There are as many as three components in most sound systems.

Speakers reproduce sound. Your vehicle probably came with speakers, but you can change them out for fancier ones if you want to.

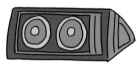

Subwoofers help to boost the bass (the lower register) of the sound being sent to the speakers. These usually have to be added to a sound system.

Amplifiers boost the power of the electrical signal from the source to the speakers to make it louder. It also translates the signal to make it more clear.

AM Radio
AM comes from a continuous signal broadcast through the air via radio waves. The degree to which that signal is amplified determines the sound.

FM Radio
FM also comes from a continuous radio signal, but its sounds are determined by slight deviations in the frequency at which the signal is broadcast.

Satellite Radio
Satellite subscription services project signals up into outer space where they are transmitted back to earth by a satellite. Cars with satellite antennae can receive these signals.

Your Own Music
You may have music on your phone, on an MP3 player, on a disc, or on a cassette tape. Your head unit may have a way to play music from these formats.

Hi, I'm Chris, and I'm the fella who wrote and drew this book.

When I was younger, I didn't know **anything** about cars, except how to drive them too fast and how to accidentally back into mailboxes.

Uh-oh.

I figured that car engines were **too complicated** to figure out. Better leave them to the experts!

But one day, when I was an adult, my car wouldn't start.

I mentioned this to a neighbor, just griping...

YOU COULD DO IT YOURSELF

Turns out that the only thing I needed to start fixing my own car was the confidence that I could. Someone telling me that I could* gave me that confidence!

By reading an online tutorial and watching a YouTube video...

great resources for car maintenance...

I changed the starter myself. My first car repair!

*And guess what? I'm telling you that **you** can, **too**!

Now I do a lot of my own repairs, and each time I learn a little more about my vehicle, how it works, and how I can help it to work **better**.

Oh no! We're supposed to be guests at a comic convention, and now we're going to be **late**!

Not if **I** have anything to say about it!

Homemade bumper with a winch plate (no winch, though)

120

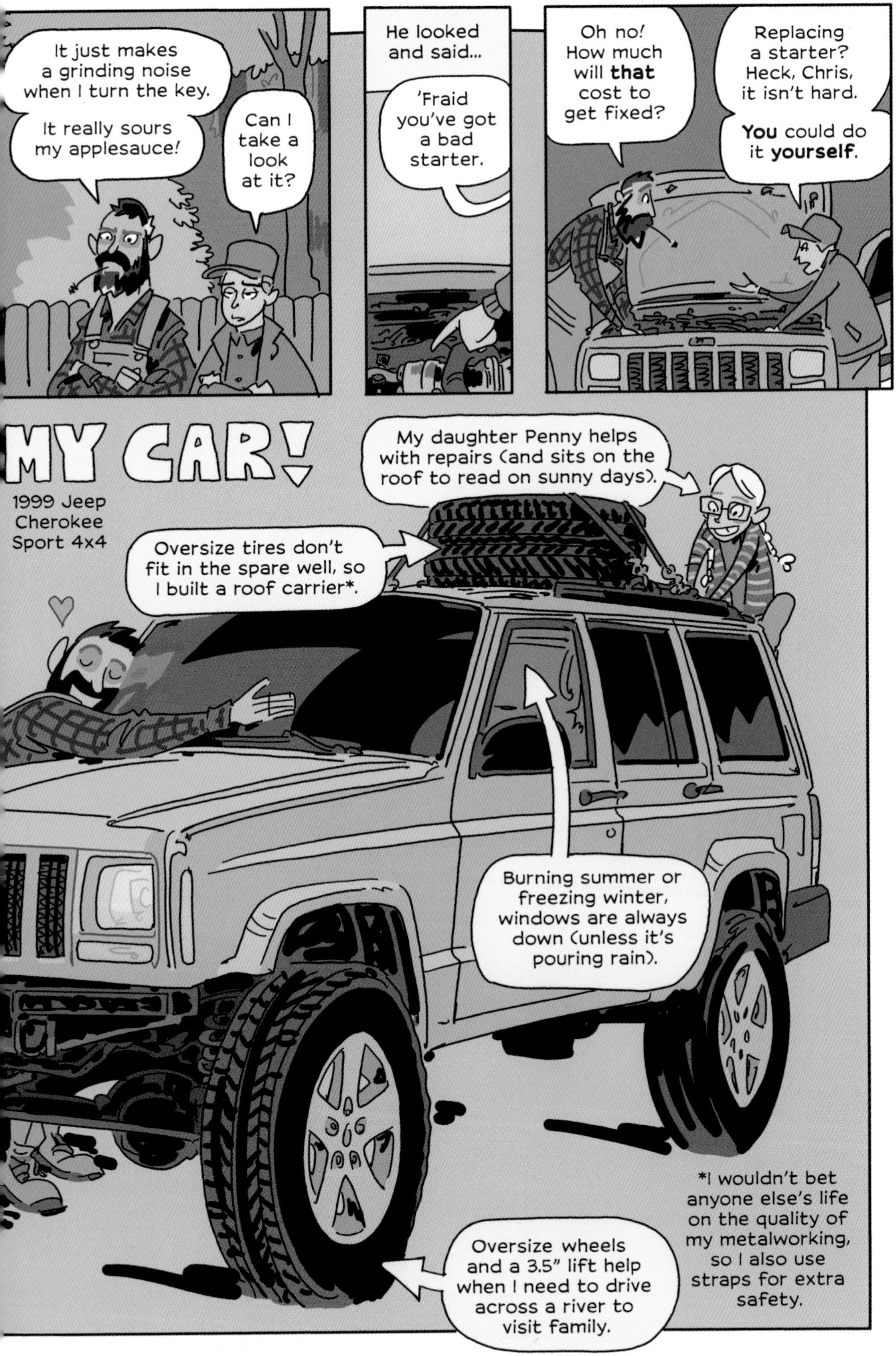
It just makes a grinding noise when I turn the key.
It really sours my applesauce!
Can I take a look at it?
He looked and said...
'Fraid you've got a bad starter.
Oh no! How much will **that** cost to get fixed?
Replacing a starter? Heck, Chris, it isn't hard.
You could do it **yourself**.
MY CAR!
1999 Jeep Cherokee Sport 4x4
My daughter Penny helps with repairs (and sits on the roof to read on sunny days).
Oversize tires don't fit in the spare well, so I built a roof carrier*.
Burning summer or freezing winter, windows are always down (unless it's pouring rain).
Oversize wheels and a 3.5" lift help when I need to drive across a river to visit family.
*I wouldn't bet anyone else's life on the quality of my metalworking, so I also use straps for extra safety.

There are tons of good books about cars and car maintenance out there, but here are a few that I've found especially useful.

Auto Mechanics Fundamentals
by Martin W. Stockel
and Martin T. Stockel

This book explains how engines work by presenting each component as the solution to a problem. It makes everything seem very practical and helps you to understand why the parts exist and what they do. This is my very top pick if you want to understand, well, the fundamentals of auto mechanics.

Saturday Mechanic and **Complete Car Care Manual**
from *Popular Mechanics*

These are handy books for understanding and fixing all sorts of problems. They've got clear illustrations and instructions and are great to have on hand.

Haynes Automotive Repair Manuals
from Haynes Publishing

The writers and illustrators of the manuals published by Haynes completely disassemble the cars that are the subject of their manuals and, in putting them back together, create a far more detailed and comprehensive guide to your specific vehicle than your owner's manual.

I keep **my** Haynes Manual in my car. You never know when you might be somewhere with no phone service, but you can reference a book **anywhere**!

Also, the internet is a great resource for car tips, process tutorials, videos, and tips from mechanics and manufacturers alike!

Happy fixing!

GET TO KNOW YOUR UNIVERSE!

SCIENCE COMICS

"An excellent addition to school and classroom libraries."
—*School Library Journal*

...And more books coming soon!

First Second

Copyright © 2019 by Chris Schweizer

All instructions included in this book are provided as a resource for parents and children.
While all due care has been taken, we recommend that an adult supervise children at
all times when following the instructions in this book. The projects in this book are not
recommended for children three years and under due to potential choking hazard. Neither
the authors nor the publisher accept any responsibility for any loss, injury, or damages
sustained by anyone resulting from the instructions contained in this book.

Published by First Second
First Second is an imprint of Roaring Brook Press,
a division of Holtzbrinck Publishing Holdings Limited Partnership
175 Fifth Avenue, New York, NY 10010
All rights reserved

Library of Congress Control Number: 2018938075

Paperback ISBN: 978-1-250-15004-2
Hardcover ISBN: 978-1-250-15003-5

Our books may be purchased in bulk for promotional, educational, or business use.
Please contact your local bookseller or the Macmillan Corporate and Premium Sales Department
at (800) 221-7945 ext. 5442 or by e-mail at MacmillanSpecialMarkets@macmillan.com.

First edition, 2019
Book design by Rob Steen
Edited by Robyn Chapman and Bethany Bryan
Expert consultants: Bob Chapman and Matthew Wright

Printed in China by 1010 Printing International Limited, North Point, Hong Kong

Penciled in Adobe Photoshop on a Wacom Cintiq. About half of the book was inked on Hammermill 100#
cover copy paper with a Faber-Castell size F Pitt pen and a chisel-point Permapaque marker,
the other half was inked in Photoshop with the pencil tool. Colored digitally in Photoshop.

Paperback: 10 9 8 7 6 5 4 3 2 1
Hardcover: 10 9 8 7 6 5 4 3 2 1